VALLEY HEROES
(PART 2)

CHARLTON ATHLETIC'S LEADING GOALSCORERS

Derek Hales — CHARLTON ATHLETIC FC
Mike Flanagan — CHARLTON ATHLETIC FC
Clive Mendonca — CHARLTON ATHLETIC FC
Jason Euell — CHARLTON ATHLETIC FC

Seasons
1969/70 - 2019/20
By
JOHN FARRELL
Illustrations by David Ramzan

To Chris & Peter
Many thanks again.
John
NOVEMBER 2020

Copyright: © John Farrell 2020

All Rights Reserved. No part of this publication may be reproduced or transmitted in any form or by any means, electronic or mechanical, including photocopy, recording, or any information storage and retrieval system, without permission from the author.

The information contained within this book is believed to be true and correct at the time of writing.

Cover image & illustrations: © David Ramzan 2020

ISBN: 9798563297937

Contents

Acknowledgements v
Introduction vii
Abbreviations and Notes viii
1969/70 Ray Treacy 1
1970/71 Ray Treacy 6
1971/72 Ray Treacy 9
1972/73 Arthur Horsfield 13
1973/74 Arthur Horsfield 17
1974/75 Derek Hales 20
1975/76 Derek Hales 24
1976/77 Mike Flanagan 28
1977/78 Mike Flanagan 32
1978/79 Martin Robinson 36
1979/80 Derek Hales 41
1980/81 Derek Hales 44
1981/82 Derek Hales & Paul Walsh 47
1982/83 Derek Hales 55
1983/84 Derek Hales 59
1984/85 Mike Flanagan 63
1985/86 John Pearson 66
1986/87 Jim Melrose 71
1987/88 Garth Crooks 77
1988/89 Paul Williams 81
1989/90 Paul Williams 85
1990/91 Robert Lee 89
1991/92 Carl Leaburn 94
1992/93 Alan Pardew 98
1993/94 Carl Leaburn 103

1994/95	David Whyte	106
1995/96	Lee Bowyer	110
1996/97	Carl Leaburn & David Whyte	115
1997/98	Clive Mendonca	121
1998/99	Clive Mendonca	125
1999/00	Andy Hunt	128
2000/01	Jonatan Johansson	133
2001/02	Jason Euell	138
2002/03	Jason Euell	141
2003/04	Jason Euell	144
2004/05	Shaun Bartlett	147
2005/06	Darren Bent	151
2006/07	Darren Bent	155
2007/08	Chris Iwelumo	159
2008/09	Nicky Bailey	164
2009/10	Deon Burton	169
2010/11	Johnnie Jackson	175
2011/12	Bradley Wright-Phillips	179
2012/13	Johnnie Jackson	184
2013/14	Yann Kermorgant & Marvin Sordell	188
2014/15	Igor Vetokele & Johann Berg Gudmundsson	197
2015/16	Johann Berg Gudmundsson	205
2016/17	Ricky Holmes	208
2017/18	Josh Magennis	213
2018/19	Lyle Taylor	218
2019/20	Lyle Taylor & Macauley Bonne	224
About the Author		231
Bibliography		232

Acknowledgements

I would like to extend my thanks to the following people.

David Ramzan has again provided excellent caricatures of the players and the cover design, as he did for Valley Heroes – Part 1. His illustrations bring the book to life and I wish that I possessed just a fraction of his artistic talent. Thank you David for sticking with me and for making this second book possible.

Christine and Peter Mayes provided me with the inspiration to start this project and to see it through to its conclusion. Christine has again used her expertise to finalise the layout and format the text and the book would not have seen the light of day without her professional assistance.

Mike Whelan for the loan of a number of Charlton Handbooks which I had missing from my collection, due to them being donated to the Club's Museum. This enabled me to complete the details for several seasons which otherwise would have been more challenging. Although Mike is a Charlton supporter and a fellow football historian, he now lives near Elgin in Scotland (and is the Editor of Elgin City's matchday programme) so the postage cost alone must have been prohibitive.

Finally, I would like to thank my wife, **Liz**, for her patience and tolerance while I researched and wrote another book. If we are still around in 2070, I hope that you will indulge me again as I write Valley Heroes - Part 3, just ensure that the wheelchair is close enough to the PC.

Introduction

Welcome to Valley Heroes – Part 2, the story of Charlton Athletic's top goal-scorers from 1970 to 2020.

This is the companion book to Valley Heroes – Part 1, which covered the Addicks' first 49 seasons as a professional club from 1920/21 to 1968/69. Published on Amazon in November 2019, it is, of course, still available !

Thanks to all those people that purchased Part 1 and for the positive comments and reviews. I hope that you will get the same pleasure from Part 2.

I am an independent author and not backed by a big publishing company so every time a reader purchases one of my books I am genuinely thrilled. If you enjoy this book please leave a review on Amazon, and if you think your friends would enjoy it, please share it with them.

Valley Heroes – Part 2 looks at the careers of the men who were top scorers for Charlton Athletic for the 51 seasons from 1969/70 to 2019/20 and, together with Part 1, completes the story of the first 100 years of Charlton's top marksmen since they turned professional in 1920.

Included are the players' career details with Charlton and their record for their other clubs in the Football League, Scottish League and, where available, non-league and other national leagues. Also included are any honours they won during their career. The season(s) that they finished as Charlton's top scorer are also examined to see how they achieved their place in the Club's history.

The next 50 years would take us to 2070. I will be 120 by then so I may have to leave Part 3 to somebody else, but in the meantime, enjoy Part 2.

John Farrell

October 2020

Abbreviations and Notes

PL	FA Premier League
FL	Football League
SL	Scottish League
NL	National League
NASL	North American Soccer League
A	Appearances
G	Goals
+	Additional appearances as a substitute
=£	Denotes an estimate of the transfer fee as it would be in today's money (2019/20).

Note 1 – The Football League Divisions in this publication are equivalent to the following present day (2019/20) Leagues and Divisions.

Football League First Division = FA Premier League (Tier 1)

Football League Second Division = Football League Championship (Tier 2)

Football League First Division* = Football League Championship (Tier 2)
(* Football League Second Division renamed First Division following the creation of the FA Premier League in 1992.)

Football League Third Division = Football League - League One (Tier 3)

Note 2 – Match results: Charlton's score is always given first.

Note 3 – All facts and statistics are correct to October 2020.

1969/70 Ray Treacy

Football League – Second Division

Leading Scorer: Ray Treacy

Football League:	27+3A	6G
FA Cup:	1+1A	1G
League Cup:	1A	0G
Total	29+4A	7G

Ray Treacy
CHARLTON ATHLETIC FC

Raymond Christopher Patrick Treacy

Born: Dublin, Republic of Ireland, 18.6.1946
Died: Dublin, Republic of Ireland, 10.4.2015

Career:
Home Farm,
West Bromwich Albion (FL 2+3A 1G)
Charlton Athletic (FL 144+5A 43G)
Swindon Town (FL 55A 16G)
Preston North End (FL 54+4A 11G)
Oldham Athletic (loan) (FL 3A 1G)
West Bromwich Albion (FL 20+1A 6G)
Shamrock Rovers
Toronto Metros/Croatia (NASL)
Drogheda United (player/manager)

Honours:
Dublin Schools
Eire Schools (2 caps)
Eire U23 (1 cap) – (with WBA)
Eire Full International (42 caps 5G) – (14 caps with Charlton)
Irish Cup winner's medal 1977/78 (with Shamrock Rovers)
League of Ireland (2A) – (with Shamrock Rovers)

Ray Treacy began his career in his native Dublin with Home Farm before being snapped up by West Bromwich Albion, signing for them as an apprentice in August 1961 and then as a professional in June 1964.

He was actually capped by the Republic of Ireland in 1966 before he had made his League debut for the Baggies.

He did eventually progress to their First Team, scoring on his debut in a 2-2 draw with Sunderland, and made five appearances in all, but being unable to gain a regular place in the side, he moved to Charlton in February 1968, with the Addicks paying a fee of £17,500 (=£305,000).

He made his League debut for the Addicks against Queens Park Rangers in a 3-3 draw at The Valley and, although he didn't score, he soon started to make an impact and netted 9 goals in his 18 appearances that season. This included a hat-trick in May when Hull City were eclipsed 5-1 in SE7 as he developed a productive partnership with fellow striker Matt Tees.

He scored another 10 goals in 1968/69, including a number of spectacular long range efforts, as the Addicks finished third in the Second Division.

Having just missed out on promotion, hopes were high at The Valley for the 1969/70 campaign. However, it turned out to be another season of struggle.

Treacy actually missed the first seven matches of the season through injury but returned to the team in September for a forgettable home 0-0 draw with Cardiff City. By this time his strike partner, Matt Tees, had been sold to Luton Town so Treacy played at inside-right, partnering the classy veteran, Ray Crawford, at centre-forward. That partnership only lasted a month as Crawford was also sold (to Colchester United).

The Addicks were struggling for form and another relegation battle was looming. Treacy did not score his first goal until November when he netted the equaliser in a 2-2 draw at Leicester City. By now he had a new strike partner, Gordon Riddick, who had been signed from Gillingham and scored on is debut at Filbert Street.

The pair combined again the following week at The Valley where Charlton recorded only their fourth win of the season with a 2-1 victory over Carlisle United. This time Riddick scored the equaliser and Treacy notched the winner.

If the fans thought that a corner had at last been turned they were to be sadly disappointed. Although the Addicks were now on a run of only one defeat in seven matches, they only won two of those games and the New Year brought a disastrous spell.

January started promisingly when Treacy netted the equaliser at Aston Villa in the FA Cup third round tie which finished 1-1. The Addicks won the replay 1-0 but in the League they lost seven consecutive matches which plunged them into the relegation mire.

That run was arrested in March when Treacy scored at Carlisle United to secure a precious point in a 1-1 draw. Three more points were gained the following week in SE7 when Aston Villa were again beaten 1-0 but this was followed by a disastrous result at Deepdale where fellow relegation candidates Preston North End inflicted a 1-4 defeat, with Treacy scoring the consolation goal.

Later that month, a disastrous 0-5 home defeat to Leicester City signaled the end of Eddie Firmani's reign as Manager and his assistant, Theo Foley, was tasked with saving Charlton's Second Division skin with only four matches remaining.

The Addicks drew their next match at home to QPR 1-1 and took a point in the next game too at Oxford United, where Treacy netted a vital equaliser in another 1-1 draw. However, a 0-3 reverse at Blackburn Rovers meant that the final home match against Bristol City fell into the "must win" category.

The omens were not good as the Addicks had been thumped 0-6 at Ashton Gate back in September. However, on the night Charlton finally found their form. Alan Campbell put them ahead and Treacy netted the second goal which ultimately saved the Club from relegation. A late goal from City had nerves jangling but the hosts saw the game out and celebrated the 2-1 victory and survival.

Charlton finished 20th and escaped relegation by two points. They only won seven matches and did not record a single away win. Ray Treacy finished top scorer with a modest seven goals, which epitomised a dismal campaign in which the Addicks only scored 35 League goals, the lowest in the Division, while conceding a hefty 76.

At least Treacy's seventh goal of the season had staved off relegation……for now.

Charlton Career:

See Season 1971/72

1970/71 Ray Treacy

Football League – Second Division

Leading Scorer: Ray Treacy

Football League: 32+1A   7G

FA Cup: 1A   0G

League Cup: 2A   1G

Total   35+1A   8G

Having just survived relegation in the previous campaign it was hoped that things could only get better. They didn't.

In the opening nine League matches of 1970/71, the Addicks failed to register a single victory. The only positive result was a 3-0 home win against Southend United in the League Cup, when Ray Treacy opened his account for the season by netting the second goal.

The first League win did not arrive until October when Swindon Town were defeated 2-1 at The Valley. Treacy missed seven consecutive matches through injury during this period but returned to the team towards the end of October and netted a vital late equaliser in the home match against Luton Town which finished 1-1.

That first League win failed to inspire an upturn in form as the next seven matches were winless. To make matters worse, inspirational midfielder Alan Campbell was sold to First Division Birmingham City for £70,000 (=£1.1m).

The second League win did arrive in late November when Cardiff City were edged out 2-1 in SE7, and then the Addicks, languishing at the bottom of the table, turned the form book on its head by beating Queens Park Rangers 4-1 at Loftus Road, with Treacy scoring a brace. It was their first away win since March 1969, a depressing run of 35 away matches without a victory.

The first half of the season had seen the Addicks win only three matches out of the 21 played. The two consecutive wins in late November also failed to ignite a recovery and they did not taste victory again until late February when Oxford United were defeated 2-0 at The Valley.

The following week Treacy scored only his fifth goal of the season in a 1-2 home defeat to Watford. A number of strikers had been drafted in during the season to partner the Irishman - Dick Plumb, Bobby Hunt and Barry Endean – but it had the same effect as rearranging the deckchairs on the Titanic.

March brought a lone victory, 1-0 against Middlesbrough at The Valley but April opened with consecutive wins, the second of which saw Treacy open the scoring on Good Friday when Norwich City were beaten 2-1 in SE7. He then scored twice as Bolton Wanderers were blitzed 4-1 at The Valley, a result which relegated the Trotters.

Charlton were not safe from the drop themselves until the penultimate game of the season, when the point from their 1-1 home draw with Sunderland secured Second Division football for another year.

It had been a close call, however, and another 20th place finish. Only eight League wins and only 41 goals scored tell their own story.

Ray Treacy was again top marksman, albeit with a modest 8 goals overall.

Charlton Career:

See Season 1971/72

1971/72   Ray Treacy

Football League – Second Division

Leading Scorer: Ray Treacy

Football League:	38A	13G
FA Cup:	2A	2G
League Cup:	3A	3G
Total	43A	18G

Despite there being little change to the playing personnel, Charlton started the 1971/72 season in good form.

An opening day 1-0 home win against Hull City, in which Treacy scored the only goal, was followed by a 5-1 victory over Peterborough United in the League Cup at The Valley with Treacy notching a brace.

Although the Addicks lost the next game at Swindon Town 1-2, Treacy was again on target, and he netted in the next match too at home to Watford which was won 2-0. He had now scored five goals in the opening four matches.

Then came a dip in form as the next four games all ended in defeat. Treacy did manage a consolation goal in the 1-2 defeat at Preston North End and another in the League Cup defeat at Bristol Rovers which also ended 1-2.

October proved to be a particularly fertile month for Treacy. He started with a goal in the 2-3 defeat at Orient and followed that up with a hat-trick in the 3-2 victory at Hull City. It was the Club's first hat-trick since May 1968 when Treacy netted a treble against the same opposition.

He then scored a penalty in the next match, a 2-2 home draw with Sunderland, and rounded the month off with another strike as Bristol City were dispatched 2-0 at The Valley.

In November he scored twice in another victory in SE7, Oxford United being defeated 3-0. By the half-way point of the season, Treacy had 15 goals to his name, and was set for his best seasonal total since he joined the Club. Charlton already had eight victories, matching the total achieved in the whole of the previous season, so things were gradually moving in the right direction.

What could possibly go wrong ?

January started with consecutive victories but the Addicks were then dumped out of the FA Cup by Tranmere Rovers, losing 2-4 in a replay at Prenton Park despite Treacy netting twice. Following that, their form dipped alarmingly and they managed only two more League wins.

The home League win on the 18th March against Swindon Town (3-1) proved to be the last victory of the season. In the last ten matches they managed only three draws and lost the rest. Treacy did manage one goal during this dreadful run, netting a consolation goal in the 1-3 defeat at Burnley.

That left the Addicks in 21st position and they were relegated to the Third Division for the first time since 1935. Ironically they had recorded more wins (12) and gained more points (33) than in the previous two seasons but their luck had finally run out.

Ray Treacy finished as top scorer with 18 goals overall, his best seasonal total for the Club. Only three of those goals came in the disastrous second half of the season.

It was inevitable that Treacy would leave the Club following relegation and in June 1972 he was sold to Swindon Town.

The deal was worth £35,000 (=£465,000) with Charlton receiving £20,000 plus Swindon striker Arthur Horsfield.

Treacy did well at The County Ground before moving to Preston North End for £30,000 (=£365,000) in December 1973. He had a brief loan spell at Oldham Athletic in March 1975 and returned to West Bromwich Albion in August 1976, where he finished his Football League career.

In 1977 he returned to Ireland to sign for Shamrock Rovers, managed by his Republic of Ireland colleague Johnny Giles, where he gained an FAI Cup winners' medal in 1978, scoring a penalty in the Final.

He had a short spell in the NASL with Toronto Metros/Croatia before embarking on a management career back in Ireland with Drogheda United (player/manager), Home Farm and Shamrock Rovers, who he led to the league title in 1994.

On retiring from the game he ran his own travel agency business in Dublin prior to his death in 2015 at the age of 68.

Charlton Career:

Seasons: 1967/68 – 1971/72

Football League: 144+5A 43G

FA Cup: 7+1A 5G

League Cup: 7A 4G

Total: 158+6A 52G

1972/73 Arthur Horsfield

Football League – Third Division

Leading Scorer: Arthur Horsfield

Football League:	46A	25G
FA Cup:	4A	2G
League Cup:	5A	2G
Total	55A	29G

Arthur Horsfield
CHARLTON ATHLETIC FC

Arthur Horsfield

Born: Newcastle-upon-Tyne, 5.7.1946

Career:
Montague & North Fenham Boys Club
Middlesbrough (FL 107+4A 51G)
Newcastle United (FL 7+2A 3G)
Swindon Town (FL 107+1A 42G)
Charlton Athletic (FL 139A 54G)
Watford (FL 78A 16G)
Dartford

Honours:
Newcastle & Northumberland Boys
England Youth v Spain Youth 1964 (with Middlesbrough)
Anglo-Italian Cup winners' medal 1969 (with Swindon Town)
Anglo-Italian Cup winners' medal 1970 (with Swindon Town)

Arthur Horsfield was born in Newcastle but made his name with Middlesbrough who he signed professional for in July 1963. He developed into a prolific marksman in the Second Division on Teesside, prompting First Division Newcastle United to pay £17,500 (=£290,000) for his signature in January 1969. He found it difficult to establish himself in their team, with the likes of Wyn Davies holding down the centre-forward position, and he moved to Second Division Swindon Town in May 1969. At the time he was Swindon's record signing, the club paying £17,000 (=£280,000).

He continued his goal-scoring exploits in Wiltshire and arrived at The Valley in June 1972 as part of the deal which took Ray Treacy to Swindon. Horsfield was valued at £15,000 (=£200,000) in the £35,000 (=£465,000) deal and he proved to be one of Theo Foley's most inspired signings.

A powerful centre-forward, he was he an excellent target-man and a lethal finisher despite lacking a bit of pace. He made his Addicks debut at Walsall and duly scored in a 2-3 defeat. He was on target again a few days later at Northampton Town in the League Cup, netting the third goal in the 3-0 victory.

He opened the scoring at Rochdale in a match which the Addicks went on to win 2-0 and then grabbed a brace as Swansea City were routed 6-0 in SE7. Horsfield now had five goals in his opening five matches and the Charlton fans had a new hero.

It proved to be no fluke either as he continued to score regularly throughout the season. In September he scored in the home matches against Mansfield Town in the League Cup (4-3), Scunthorpe United (2-0), Notts County (6-1) and Watford (2-1) to bring his total to nine goals.

In October, Plymouth Argyle were defeated 3-0 at The Valley with Horsfield opening the scoring, and he then netted both goals in the 2-0 victory at Grimsby Town. A 4-2 home victory over Oldham Athletic again saw "King Arthur" score a brace.

November brought a consolation goal in the 1-3 defeat at Notts County, as they gained revenge for the earlier 6-1 mauling at The Valley. He then scored in the FA Cup first round tie at Tonbridge, netting an early goal to settle the nerves and paving the way for a 5-0 victory. He rounded the month off by scoring the equaliser in the home game with Brentford which enabled the Addicks to go on to win 2-1.

December dawned with another FA Cup goal as Horsfield netted a last minute winner at Walsall in the second round to enable the Addicks to advance with a 2-1 victory. He then scored at home to eventual champions Bolton Wanderers, who left with the points as the Addicks went down 2-3. In the next match at Bristol Rovers he gave the visitors a half-time lead but that evaporated in the second-half as Rovers hit back to inflict a 1-2 defeat.

At the half way point of the season, Horsfield had already netted 20 goals. He started the New Year well too, scoring the winner in the 1-0 home win against Rochdale and the equaliser in the 1-1 draw at York City.

But then the goals dried up during February along with the Addicks' early season form. However, March saw Horsfield back to his best and he scored in four consecutive matches – firstly at home against Halifax Town (1-0) and Grimsby Town (1-1), then away to Oldham Athletic (1-0) and Wrexham (2-2). He rounded the month off by scoring in the 1-1 draw with AFC Bournemouth in SE7.

As the season wound down in April, Horsfield added two more goals to his tally, netting against Wrexham at The Valley in a 2-1 win and at Watford in a 1-1 draw.

Charlton, following a promising start, finished in a disappointing 11th position in the Third Division table. However, Arthur Horsfield enjoyed a magnificent season, playing in all 55 matches and netting 29 goals. It was the highest total by a Charlton player since Johnny Summers achieved the same tally in 1957/58.

It was therefore no surprise when "King Arthur" was crowned Player of the Year.

Charlton Career:

See Season 1973/74

1973/74   Arthur Horsfield

Football League – Third Division

Leading Scorer: Arthur Horsfield

Football League: 46A   19G

FA Cup: 1A   0G

League Cup: <u>2A   1G</u>

                    Total   49A   20G

The Addicks made a dreadful start to the 1973/74 season, losing their opening match at home to York City 2-4. They made amends a few days later in the League Cup by defeating Brighton & Hove Albion 2-1 at the Goldstone Ground, with Arthur Horsfield netting the winner.

He scored in each of the next four matches too – at Bristol Rovers (1-2), home to Hereford United when he netted twice (2-0), home to Blackburn Rovers (4-3) and away to Brighton & Hove Albion (2-1). The victory over Blackburn also featured a young striker who scored on his debut – Derek Hales.

In October, Horsfield scored a brace at The Valley as Halifax Town were demolished 5-2. Hales also netted twice. Later in the month the two combined again in the 3-0 defeat of Rochdale in SE7 with Horsfield adding the third goal following a brace by Hales. Horsfield then hit the equaliser at Blackburn Rovers in a 1-1 draw.

His next strike came in late November at The Valley in a victory over Plymouth Argyle (2-0), and a week later he netted twice in another Valley victory, 2-0 against Port Vale.

His final goal of the calendar year came at Hereford United as he notched the third goal in a 3-2 victory. At the half way point of the season his total stood at 14 goals.

In January, Horsfield scored at The Valley as Huddersfield Town were edged out 2-1, but in February he hit a rare barren patch before hitting four goals during March. These strikes all came on home soil against – Southend United (2-1), Cambridge United (2-0) and Oldham Athletic (4-1) when he netted twice.

His final goal of the season came in the penultimate match at Oldham Athletic, where his early goal set up a 2-0 victory.

The Addicks finished mid-table again, this time in 14th position in what was another season of underachievement,

Arthur Horsfield was top scorer with 20 goals and he was again ever-present, playing in all 49 League and cup matches.

The following season, 1974/75, Horsfield was a key component in the team that at last achieved promotion back to the Second Division. He was eclipsed in the goal-scoring stakes by Derek Hales, who notched 21, but "King Arthur" still netted 12 times despite playing at centre-half in 23 matches. He was ever-present yet again, playing in all 50 matches.

Having got Charlton back into the Second Division, Horsfield only played in the first match back in the second tier before being sold to Watford for £20,000 (=£170,000) in September 1975.

He gave the Hornets good service before winding down his career with Dartford, who he joined in September 1977.

Arthur Horsfield gave Charlton magnificent service over three seasons. Not only did he score 61 goals, he also set a Club record which is unlikely ever to be beaten by playing in 156 consecutive matches.

That was quite some signing by Theo Foley.

Charlton Career:

Seasons: 1972/73 – 1975/76

Football League: 139A 54G

FA Cup: 7A 3G

League Cup: 10A 4G

Total: 156A 61G

1974/75   Derek Hales

Football League – Third Division

Leading Scorer: Derek Hales

Football League: 44A   20G

FA Cup: 2A   0G

League Cup: 2A   1G

Total   48A   21G

Derek David Hales

Born: Lower Halstow, Kent, 15.12.1951

Career:
Upchurch Minors
Bridge Rovers,
Gillingham (youth)
Faversham Town
Dartford,
Luton Town (FL 5+2A 1G)
Charlton Athletic (FL 126+3A 72G)
Derby County (FL 22+1A 4G)
West Ham United (FL 23+1A 10G)
Charlton Athletic (FL 186+5A 76G)
Gillingham (FL 31+9A 9G)

Honours:
Rainham Schools

Derek Hales sprang to prominence with Dartford where his impressive scoring record prompted Luton Town to sign him in March 1972. He scored on his League debut for the Hatters but was unable to establish a regular place in their team.

Theo Foley was also an admirer and managed to bring the young striker to The Valley, initially on loan, in July 1973. Following an impressive three months, Charlton managed to sign Hales for £4000 (=£48,000) in October 1973 and he turned out to be one of the most significant signings in the Club's history.

Hales netted eight times in his first season, including a goal on his debut, but it was in 1974/75 that he really started to show the talent that he possessed.

By this time his mentor, Theo Foley, had left the Club and been replaced by Andy Nelson from Gillingham, who was tasked with getting the Addicks back to the Second Division. He had achieved promotion with Gillingham the previous season from the Fourth Division.

Charlton started the campaign at Halifax Town and returned with a point following a 2-2 draw. Hales opened his account by netting the second goal. He was on target again a few days later in the League Cup, his opening goal paving the way to a 4-0 victory against Peterborough United at The Valley.

His next strike came in September at Brighton & Hove Albion in a 2-1 win but he then hit top form in October by scoring in five successive matches – at home to Tranmere Rovers (3-3) and Peterborough United (3-0), away at Bury (1-2), then in the home victories over Chesterfield (3-2) and Watford (4-1).

The run was halted when he missed the next two matches through injury, but he returned to action at Watford and duly scored in a 2-0 win. Later in November he netted a brace as Walsall were dispatched 4-2 in SE7 and he also scored in the home victory over, eventual champions, Blackburn Rovers which finished 2-1.

By the halfway point of the season, Charlton were well placed towards the top end of the table and the predatory Hales had netted 12 times.

In January he only scored once but it was a goal of some significance. Crystal Palace, local rivals who were also involved in the promotion race, visited The Valley at the end of the month. Hales netted the decisive goal to seal a vital 1-0 win for the Addicks.

He then experienced an eight game barren spell, although there was only one defeat during that run, but he bounced back to form in March by hitting a hat-trick in the 3-1 home victory against Halifax Town. All three goals coming in the opening 20 minutes. The next match also finished 3-1 to the Addicks, with Hales notching the third goal at Huddersfield Town.

As April dawned, Charlton's push for promotion started to stall. They opened the month with two defeats, the second of these was to AFC Bournemouth in SE7 when Hales scored in the 2-3 reverse. He then netted a very welcome winner to secure a 1-0 victory at Tranmere Rovers.

There were still five games left but the Addicks only managed to get two points from four of them, thus moving the final home match against Preston North End into the "must win" category.

Nearly 25,000 fans packed into The Valley on the Tuesday night hoping to see promotion clinched at last. Preston had not read the script, however, and took an early lead. Bob Curtis then had a penalty saved and the omens were not good.

But in the second-half, Charlton staged a recovery. Bob Goldthorpe equalised and then Hales stepped up, scoring twice to secure a 3-1 victory, third place, and promotion back the Second Division.

Derek Hales finished the season with a total of 21 goals and The Valley had a new hero.

He had established himself as a lethal finisher and his pace over ten yards and his sheer aggression made him deadly in the penalty area. Perhaps this was alluded to by his nickname on the terraces, "Killer", although I doubt that even he would have gone that far.

Charlton Career:

See Season 1983/84

1975/76   Derek Hales

Football League – Second Division

Leading Scorer: Derek Hales

Football League: 40A   28G

FA Cup: 4A   0G

League Cup: <u>6A   3G</u>

Total   50A   31G

As the Addicks kicked off their first season back in the second tier for three years, the question was could Derek Hales maintain his goal-scoring form at the higher level. The answer was an emphatic "yes"!

Although Charlton started the season with two defeats, they gradually settled into their new surroundings. Hales netted his first goal in September in the 1-1 home draw with Blackpool and followed that up a few days later in the League Cup second round replay at Oxford United when he scored in extra time in a 1-1 draw to take the tie to a second replay.

He then notched the decisive goal as Hull City were edged out 1-0 in SE7 before scoring the winner at Oxford United in the second replay of the League Cup. Hales scored twice, his second goal coming in extra time to take the Addicks through 3-2.

October opened with two heavy defeats for the Addicks but they then went unbeaten for the rest of the month with Hales scoring in four successive matches. He grabbed a brace as Oldham Athletic were beaten in South London (3-1) and netted twice again at York City in another 3-1 victory. A goal at Carlisle United in a 1-1 draw was followed by another double in the 4-1 thumping of Southampton at The Valley. That was seven goals in four matches for Charlton's bearded talisman.

However, November and December were not good months for Charlton or Hales as only two wins were recorded. "Killer" managed one goal in the home defeat to Sunderland (1-2) in a match where the frustrated striker was sent off towards the end. However, he bounced back in the last match of the year, scoring twice in the 3-2 defeat of Chelsea at Stamford Bridge.

In January he netted twice as Bristol Rovers were swept aside 3-0 at The Valley and in February he hit a hat-trick against Fulham in another home victory, 3-2, with his winner coming in second half injury time.

In the next match Hales found himself having to takeover in goal at Sunderland, when keeper, Graham Tutt, received a serious injury, which ultimately finished his career. The makeshift keeper could not prevent the Addicks going down to a 1-4 defeat.

Normal service was then resumed as Hales netted four goals in the next three matches. Two came at home to Nottingham Forest (2-2) followed by a single strike against Carlisle United (4-2), also at The Valley. He then scored the only goal in the 1-0 win at Orient.

At the end of March, he hit another rich vein of form, hitting five goals in four matches. It started with the equaliser at Luton Town (1-1) followed by another strike at Hull City (2-2). On Good Friday he was on target as West Bromwich Albion were beaten 2-1 back in SE7. He then hit a brace at Southampton but he couldn't prevent the Addicks slipping to a 2-3 defeat.

His final goals of the season came at Portsmouth where Charlton came back from 0-2 down to grab a 2-2 draw, as Hales hit another brace.

Charlton finished in a very satisfactory ninth place in their first season back in the Second Division.

Derek Hales enjoyed a magnificent season, scoring 31 goals, only two short of Ralph Allen's Club record 33 in 1934/35, and he was voted Player of the Year.

He was also the top scorer in the Second Division…and there was still more to come.

The following season, 1976/77, Hales continued his prolific scoring form. By December 1976 he had netted an amazing 18 goals in 19 appearances and the interest from First Division clubs was increasing game by game. It was almost inevitable that Charlton would cash in on their prize asset and eventually a bid was accepted from Derby County. The fee sounded like a bingo callers nightmare – "All the three's" - £333,333 (=£2.4m) which was a new record for Charlton for an outgoing transfer.

Hales' departure for First Division football at the Baseball Ground left the Addicks with a huge hole to fill and ended any realistic ambitions of promotion for the foreseeable future.

Hales had scored an eye-watering 78 goals for the Addicks in three and half seasons but it wouldn't be the last that the Valley faithful would see of him.

Charlton Career:

See Season 1983/84

1976/77   Mike Flanagan

Football League – Second Division

Leading Scorer: Mike Flanagan

Football League: 42A   23G

FA Cup: 2A   0G

League Cup: 3A   0G

Total   47A   23G

Michael Anthony Flanagan

Born: Ilford, Essex, 9.11.1952

Career:
Tottenham Hotspur (amateur)
Charlton Athletic (FL 241+13A 85G)
New England Tea Men (Loan) (NASL 29A 30G)
Crystal Palace (FL 56A 8G)
Queens Park Rangers (FL 71+7A 20G)
Charlton Athletic (FL 89+4A 24G)
Cambridge United FL 7+2A 3G)
Margate

Honours:
FA Youth Cup winner's medal 1970 (with Tottenham Hotspur)
England Amateur Youth 1971 – 3 caps (with Tottenham Hotspur)
England 'B' – 3 caps 1G (2 caps with Charlton)
NASL Most Valuable Player 1978 (with New England Tea Men)
FA Cup runners-up medal 1982 (with QPR)
Second Division runners-up 1985/86 (with Charlton Athletic)

Mike Flanagan was another of Theo Foley's inspired signings. He arrived at The Valley, on trial, in July 1971 from Tottenham Hotspur and was signed as a professional a month later on a free transfer.

He was used mainly as a winger in the early part of his career but he proved that he was also an effective central striker, especially when he netted four times as Notts County were dismantled 6-1 at The Valley in September 1972.

He was the Club's second highest scorer (behind Arthur Horsfield) in 1972/73 and 1973/74 and he was second only to Hales in 1975/76.

The 1976/77 season saw Flanagan develop a prolific partnership with Hales as the pair formed a potent combination as twin strikers. Another shrewd Theo Foley signing, Colin Powell, was operating on the right-wing and supplied the crosses for the deadly duo.

Flanagan's first goal of the season came in September at Hereford United where the Addicks prevailed 2-1, and he then netted a brace back in SE7 as Southampton were blitzed 6-2. He also scored in a third successive match, at Carlisle United, where the Addicks went down 2-4.

In October, his strike partner, Hales, scored a memorable hat-trick against Hull City at The Valley which finished 3-1. The match highlights were shown on ITV and the second goal was later voted Goal of the Season.

Meanwhile, Flanagan continued to enhance his own striking reputation by scoring in the next four matches, starting at Burnley where the Addicks surrendered a 4-1 lead to draw 4-4. He then netted in the home 3-2 victory over Sheffield United, the away draw at Bristol Rovers (1-1), and the 3-1 Valley victory against Plymouth Argyle.

His next goals came in December in the 4-0 home victory against Blackburn Rovers. Flanagan netted twice, but the win was bitter-sweet as it marked the last appearance of Derek Hales who was sold to First Division Derby County a week later. So Charlton's strike force was broken up at a time where the pair had plundered 28 goals between them (Hales 18, Flanagan 10).

The next match was at local rivals Millwall where youngster Tony Burman was given his League debut in place of Hales. Burman obliged by netting a late equaliser in a 1-1 draw. Perhaps the Addicks could still prosper without their striking ace.

Flanagan also stepped up and scored in successive home victories in January. He netted twice against Bristol Rovers (4-3) and then opened the scoring against Nottingham Forest (2-1).

February saw him on target at Fulham, in a 1-1 draw, and in the 2-0 defeat of Orient back in SE7. He then went seven matches without a goal but hit form again over Easter. On Good Friday he opened the scoring in the local derby against Millwall at The Valley, his strike paving the way to a 3-2 victory. In another London derby against Chelsea on Easter Monday, he hit a hat-trick in another home win (4-0).

His early goal at Blackpool in the next match set the Addicks on their way to a 2-0 lead at the interval. However, a late capitulation saw them having to settle for a point as the match ended 2-2.

He rounded off the season with a brace in the 5-2 demolition of Burnley at The Valley and then scored in the last match of the season at Notts County, netting the only goal in the 1-0 victory.

Flanagan finished the campaign with 23 goals, all scored in the League, and he played in all 47 League cup matches. He succeeded Derek Hales as top scorer and also as Player of the Year.

Charlton improved their League position, finishing seventh, but it could have been so much better had the Hales-Flanagan partnership been allowed to continue and flourish.

Charlton Career:

See Season 1984/85

1977/78 Mike Flanagan

Football League – Second Division

Leading Scorer: Mike Flanagan

Football League: 32A 16G

FA Cup: 1A 0G

League Cup: <u>1A 1G</u>

Total 34A 17G

As the 1977/78 season got underway, there was still no sign of an experienced replacement for Derek Hales. The latest solution to be tried was Lawrie Abrahams from non-league Barking to partner Mike Flanagan up front.

Flanagan opened his account in the second match, scoring twice in the 3-1 home win against Blackpool. Just days later he was on target again in the League Cup, putting Charlton ahead with a penalty against Wrexham at The Valley. However, two late goals from the Red Dragons sent the Addicks spinning out of the competition (1-2).

Worse was to come as in the next match, at Luton Town, the hosts put seven goals past the Addicks ! Flanagan's late penalty provided scant consolation in the 1-7 thrashing.

Thankfully there followed an upturn in form and a five match unbeaten run. Flanagan hit four goals in three consecutive matches, netting at Oldham Athletic (1-1), at Millwall (1-1) and then a brace as Bristol Rovers were beaten 3-1 back in South London.

His highlight of the season came in October when promotion favourites Tottenham Hotspur visited The Valley. Flanagan did his old club no favours and netted a second-half hat-trick as Charlton triumphed 4-1.

November heralded another prolific period for the striker as he scored in five consecutive games. The sequence started with a goal in the 2-2 home draw with Mansfield Town and he then scored at Bolton Wanderers in a 1-2 defeat. Back at The Valley, Sheffield United were defeated 3-0 with Flanagan again on target, and he then scored at Hull City in a 2-0 victory. Finally he netted the winner back in SE7 as Sunderland were edged out 3-2.

It was now into December and, eventual champions, Bolton Wanderers visited The Valley just before Christmas. Flanagan hit the winner as the Addicks sent them home pointless by registering a valuable 2-1 victory.

Flanagan had now scored 17 goals and Charlton were in mid-table but there was then a disastrous drop in form which saw the Addicks fighting another relegation battle.

Following the win against Bolton, Charlton went 13 matches without a victory, which included an early exit from the FA Cup. The sequence was not broken until late March when a 1-0 home victory over Crystal Palace stopped the rot.

Flanagan, however, gained his first, of three, England 'B' caps in February against West Germany as his striking talent began to be recognised beyond the confines of South London.

Also in February, Charlton had announced a twinning with North American club, New England Tea Men, which resulted in a number of players being switched to the States before the English season was over. Flanagan, Abrahams and Colin Powell were the players chosen to make the trip in early April. It was a bizarre decision as Charlton still had five matches to play and were not mathematically certain of staying up.

They only recorded one win in those final matches and had to get a point from their last game at Orient to avoid the drop. A 0-0 draw did the trick but it had been a desperately close call.

Charlton finished 17th in a season which was definitely one of two halves. Flanagan finished as top scorer, with 17 goals, all scored between August and December.

His move to the States proved successful though, and he netted 30 goals in 29 NASL matches and was voted the league's Most Valuable Player for 1978.

However, he was back at The Valley for the start of the 1978/79 season where he was reunited with the returning Derek Hales. All went well until the pair were famously sent off for fighting each other in an FA Cup tie with Maidstone United in January 1979.

There must have been some bad feeling between them with Flanagan assuming Hales' goal-scoring mantle during his absence. Whatever the reason, the incident led to Flanagan leaving the Club in August 1979 when he joined Crystal Palace for a fee of £650,000 (=£3.3m) to pursue his career in the First Division.

It was a terrible loss to Charlton, to lose a striker who had netted 95 goals during his eight seasons at the Club. However, like Hales, he would return to The Valley later in his career.

Charlton Career:

See Season 1984/85

1978/79   Martin Robinson

Football League – Second Division

Leading Scorer: Martin Robinson

Football League: 35A   15G

FA Cup: 2A   1G

League Cup: <u>4A   3G</u>

Total   41A   19G

Martin John Robinson

Born: Ilford, Essex, 17.7.1957

Career:
Tottenham Hotspur (FL 5+1A 2G)
Charlton Athletic (FL 218+10A 58G)
Reading (loan) (FL 6A 2G)
Gillingham (FL 91+5A 23G)
Southend United (FL 43+13A 14G)
Cambridge United (FL 7+9A 1G)
Enfield

Honours:
Thurrock & District Schools

Martin Robinson came through the youth system at Tottenham Hotspur and was signed as a professional by them in May 1975. He found it difficult to establish a regular place in their first team and eventually moved to Charlton in February 1978 for a £15,000 (=£86,000) fee.

He scored on his League debut at Bristol Rovers in a 2-2 draw, and in his 16 appearances that season (1977/78) he scored seven times.

In 1978/79 he was in competition with Hales and Flanagan for the striking positions and played some of the early matches on the wing in support of the dynamic duo. He scored his first goal in August in the League Cup at Colchester United, where the Addicks triumphed 3-2, and the following month he hit both goals in the 2-1 League win at Blackburn Rovers.

He hit another brace in the League Cup at Chesterfield as the Addicks triumphed by the incredible score-line of 5-4.

Following an injury to Hales, Robinson was moved up front to partner

Flanagan and fortunately he proved a success as Hales was eventually out of action for three months. In October he scored twice in an impressive 4-1 home victory over Newcastle United and also scored at Cardiff City where the Addicks again triumphed 4-1.

Another high-scoring game in November, saw Robinson net a double at Bristol Rovers in a 5-5 draw and he was on target in the next match too at home to Luton Town. Unfortunately his first-half strike was eclipsed by two Hatters' goals in the second-half as the Addicks succumbed 1-2.

December brought just one goal, and that was only a late consolation in a 1-6 drubbing at Preston North End. Hales then returned to fitness and replaced Robinson, who moved to the subs bench, for the last match of the year.

January 1979 was not a month that the Club would care to remember. Not only were no League games played due to the bad weather, it also brought the infamous FA Cup third round tie with non-league Maidstone United at The Valley. On a night when the Addicks struggled against their part-time opponents, frustrations boiled over as both Hales and Flanagan were sent off for fighting….each other ! The final result of 1-1 was a mere footnote to a truly miserable evening for the Club.

The fallout from that incident resulted in Charlton losing the services of Hales for a period (he was sacked, reinstated and fined) and Flanagan permanently (he walked out when Hales was reinstated) and was eventually transferred to Crystal Palace.

So the Club lost two quality strikers and it was up to the likes of Martin Robinson to step into the breach. Having not been involved in the first Maidstone debacle, he led the attack in the replay at London Road and scored the second goal which edged Charlton through 2-1.

February at last saw some League games played and Robinson scored in the first one at Notts County (1-1) and then in the home win over Blackburn Rovers (2-0). In those matches he partnered Flanagan up front but, when Hales was reinstated, Flanagan walked out and Robinson partnered Hales for the rest of the season. What a mess.

March brought another high-scoring match at St James' Park as Newcastle United gained revenge by inflicting a 3-5 defeat on the Addicks. Robinson notched the third goal to make the final score a bit more respectable.

His penultimate goal of the season came in another defeat, 1-2 at Orient but he finished the season with a flourish. Going into the last match, Charlton had to win to ensure their Second Division safety and it was Robinson who stepped up, scoring twice to defeat Oldham Athletic 2-0 at The Valley.

Charlton finished 19th and avoided relegation by one point.

Throughout the turmoil of the season, Martin Robinson was one of the few rays of hope. He finished top scorer with 19 goals and proved what an excellent signing he had been.

He continued to give the Club good service for the next five years. He had a loan spell at Reading in September 1982 and eventually left The Valley in October 1984 to sign for Gillingham who paid a fee of £15,500 (=£50,000).

Following a successful period at Priestfield, he moved to Southend United in July 1987 for £25,000 (=£70,000) before joining his last League club, Cambridge United, in June 1989. He finished his senior career at Enfield.

Martin Robinson was a popular figure at The Valley, and scored on his debut for the Club in all three competitions – League, League Cup and FA Cup. In total he netted 67 goals.

He also achieved the holy grail - scoring 100 goals in a League career spanning over 400 games.

Charlton Career:

Seasons: 1977/78 – 1984/85

Football League: 218+10A 58G

FA Cup: 8+1A 3G

League Cup: 16+3A 6G

Total: 242+14A 67G

1979/80   Derek Hales

Football League – Second Division

Leading Scorer: Derek Hales

Football League:	23A	8G
FA Cup:	1A	0G
League Cup:	2A	1G
Total	26A	9G

Derek Hales rejoined Charlton in July 1979.

His big money move to Derby County had not really worked out, partly due to playing in a Derby team that was in decline following their glory days under Brian Clough. He was transferred to West Ham United in September 1977, the Hammers paying a fee of £110,000 (=£688,000). He had a decent season at Upton Park, scoring 10 goals in the First Division in only 24 outings, but in July 1978 Charlton came in with a bid to bring him back to The Valley. The Addicks paid their then record fee of £75,500 (=£436,000).

He netted nine goals (in 24 outings) in his first season back (1978/79) and then became the Club's top scorer, for a third time, in 1979/80 in what turned out to be a dire campaign for the Addicks.

The season started badly and gradually got worse. The first match was in the League Cup at Peterborough United where the Addicks went down 1-3 in the first leg of the first round tie. In the second leg back in SE7, Hales scored to reduce the deficit but a late Posh equaliser saw the Addicks exit the competition 2-4 on aggregate.

The opening three League matches only yielded two points from two draws but Hales scored in the next match at Orient which also finished level 1-1. He also gave Charlton the lead in the next game, at home to Wrexham, but two second-half goals from the Welshmen inflicted a home defeat 1-2.

An injury then kept him out of the next 10 matches, only three of which were won, but he returned to the team in November for the match at Chelsea where the Addicks suffered another defeat (1-3).

During October, former captain Mike Bailey returned to the Club as Chief Coach with Andy Nelson being reclassified as General Manager. However, it was not clear who held the responsibility for team selection.

Charlton were by now deeply embroiled in a relegation battle so there were two very welcome home wins in December against West Ham United (1-0) and Leicester City (2-0) with Hales scoring in the latter.

But if the fans thought that things were improving, they were to be sadly mistaken. Following the Leicester game, the Addicks went nine League games without a win. They were also dumped out of the FA Cup at Wrexham, who scored six goals without reply!

The next win did not arrive until March 1st when Bristol Rovers were beaten 4-0 at The Valley, with Hales netting his fifth goal of the season. He also scored in the next match at Cardiff City but it was only a consolation in a 1-3 defeat.

His next strike came at Oldham Athletic in a high-scoring encounter. Despite Hales scoring a penalty and the Addicks netting three goals, they still went down 3-4.

At the end of March, Andy Nelson left the Club "by mutual consent", leaving Mike Bailey in sole charge as Manager.

On Good Friday, Hales scored a late consolation goal at The Valley as the Addicks slumped to yet another defeat, losing 1-4 to Luton Town. His last goal of the season came in the final match at West Ham United which also ended 1-4. By that time Charlton had been well and truly relegated.

The Addicks were winless in the last 12 matches of the season, in fact, that 4-0 victory over Bristol Rovers was their only win in the second half of the campaign. They finished bottom of the table in 22nd place with only 22 points, their lowest points total since 1956/57, when they were also relegated. Only six wins were achieved and none away from home. It was a truly disastrous campaign.

Hales missed nearly half of the League matches with injury so his 8 goals in 23 appearances was a reasonable return. Overall he scored 9 times in 26 outings.

Charlton Career:

See Season 1984/85

1980/81   Derek Hales

Football League – Third Division

Leading Scorer: Derek Hales

Football League: 39+1A   17G

FA Cup: 5A   4G

League Cup: <u>4A   2G</u>

Total   48+1A   23G

As Charlton prepared for their first season back in the Third Division for five years, Manager Mike Bailey put a new strike force in place.

Youth graduate Paul Walsh, who had made his debut during the previous campaign, was selected to start alongside the experienced Derek Hales. It proved to be an inspired decision.

The season opened with the League Cup first round matches. Charlton visited Brentford for the first leg but came away 1-3 down despite Walsh giving them the lead. In the second leg back in SE7, it was a different story as a Walsh hat-trick and a Hales double blitzed the Bees 5-0. The Addicks went through 6-3 on aggregate and it marked the start of a fruitful partnership.

Brentford were also the visitors to The Valley for the first League game. Hales was on target as the Addicks clinched the points with a 3-1 win. His next strike also came in SE7 when he netted a penalty to defeat Chester 1-0.

The Addicks then hit a lean spell, losing three games in succession, although Hales was on target at home to Colchester United with a penalty (1-2), and at Exeter City (3-4).

Charlton then went on an amazing run of 17 League and cup matches without defeat from the beginning of October. Included in that run was a new Club record of seven consecutive victories.

Hales was in fine form during this run, scoring in four consecutive games in October – home to Sheffield United (2-0), at Hull City (2-0), at Swindon Town where he hit a brace (3-0), and finally at home to Blackpool (2-1).

November was no different as he netted in three successive games – at Walsall (2-2), home to Rotherham United (2-0), and home to Newport County (3-0).

Next came the FA Cup first round tie away to non-league Harlow Town. A cup shock was avoided as Hales was on target in a 2-0 win.

Into December, and Hales hit a vital winner at Gillingham (1-0) and then turned his attention to the FA Cup again. Charlton had been drawn at home to AFC Bournemouth and late goals from Walsh and Hales took them through to the third round 2-1.

Boxing Day saw the long unbeaten run come to an end when the Addicks slipped to a 0-1 defeat at Oxford United. But it proved to be only a blip as they were undefeated in the next six games.

Hales was on target in four successive matches again – in the FA Cup he scored a late winner at Plymouth Argyle (2-1), in the League at home to Hull City (3-2), away at Chesterfield (1-0), and in the FA Cup fourth round at Fulham where he again hit the winner in a 2-1 victory.

His next strike came in March at Sheffield United in a 2-3 defeat and his final goal of the season came at the end of that month, when the Addicks won 3-1 at Reading.

As April dawned, the wheels seemed to be coming off the Addicks' promotion bandwagon. They suddenly lost four consecutive games but they turned things around and clinched promotion by winning 2-1 at Carlisle United in the penultimate match. The final match at The Valley saw them put the proverbial icing on the promotion cake by defeating Gillingham 2-1.

Charlton finished in third place to gain promotion back the Second Division. Hales finished with 23 goals and became the Club's top scorer for a fourth time. He was ably supported by Walsh with 18 and Martin Robinson with 13.

What a difference a year makes.

Charlton Career:

See Season 1984/85

1981/82   Derek Hales & Paul Walsh

Football League – Second Division

Leading Scorers: Derek Hales & Paul Walsh

Derek Hales

Football League:	35A	11G
FA Cup:	1A	0G
League Cup:	<u>4A</u>	<u>2G</u>
Total	40A	13G

As Charlton prepared to kick-off their first season back in the Second Division, they did so with a new Manager.

Having lead the Addicks to promotion, Mike Bailey was offered, and accepted, the Manager's job at First Division Brighton & Hove Albion. Their previous Manager, Alan Mullery, had left the Seagulls and was then appointed to the vacant position at The Valley.

The other significant change was the introduction of 3 points for a win in the Football League.

The opening League fixture ended in defeat at Luton Town (0-3) in a match in which no fewer than six Mullery signings made their Charlton debuts. The next match was in the League Cup at Reading and the Addicks came away with a 2-2 draw from the first leg, with Derek Hales opening his account for the season, equalising with a late penalty.

He scored in the second leg too as Charlton won 3-1, after extra time, to go through 5-3 on aggregate.

His next goals came in October when he netted a brace to see off Derby County in SE7 (2-1), and he then netted the equaliser in the next match at Shrewsbury Town which finished 1-1.

Going into November, the Addicks hit a lean streak, losing five matches in a row. Hales was still scoring though and notched single strikes at home to Queens Park Rangers (1-2), at Rotherham United (1-2) and at home to Chelsea (3-4).

In December he scored at Watford, where the Addicks came back from 0-2 down to take a point in a 2-2 draw, and he then netted the winner at Cardiff City as all three points came back to The Valley following a 1-0 win.

By the end of the year, Hales had netted 10 goals but the second half of the season was not as productive.

January opened with a 2-0 win at Blackburn Rovers with Hales netting the first goal, and he also scored the opener later in the month at Grimsby Town where the Addicks fought out an entertaining 3-3 draw.

He was to score just once more, in March, when he put Charlton ahead at Leicester City, but three late goals from the hosts saw the Addicks go down 1-3.

That defeat came during the poor run at the end of the season when the last 11 games yielded only one win and eight defeats. Hales missed the last five matches but still finished as joint top scorer (with Paul Walsh) with 13 goals – the fifth time he had topped the Club's scoring charts.

Hales had now scored 132 goals for the Club and was closing in on Stuart Leary's record of 163.

Despite the poor end to the season, the Addicks finished in a comfortable 13th position so they had at least consolidated their place back in the second tier.

Charlton Career:

See Season 1984/85

Paul Walsh

Football League:	38A	13G
FA Cup:	1A	0G
League Cup:	4A	0G
Total	43A	13G

Paul Walsh
CHARLTON ATHLETIC FC

Paul Anthony Walsh

Born: Plumstead, London, 1.10.1962

Career:
Charlton Athletic (FL 85+2A 24G)
Luton Town (FL 80A 25G)
Liverpool (FL 63+14A 25G)
Tottenham Hotspur (FL 84+44A 19G)
Queens Park Rangers (loan) (FL 2A 0G)
Portsmouth (FL 67+6A 14G)
Manchester City (PL 53A 16G)
Portsmouth (FL 21A 5G)

Honours:
England Youth - 10 caps (with Charlton Athletic)
England U21 – 4 caps (with Luton Town)
England Full International – 5 caps 1G (with Luton Town)
PFA Young Player of the Year 1984 (with Luton Town)
First Division Championship medal 1985/86 (with Liverpool)
Football League Super Cup winner' medal 1986 (with Liverpool)
FA Charity Shield runners-up medal 1984 (with Liverpool)
European Super Cup runners-up medal 1984 (with Liverpool)
First Division runners-up 1984/85 (with Liverpool)
First Division runners-up 1986/87 (with Liverpool)
European Cup runners-up medal 1984/85 (with Liverpool)
Football League Cup runners-up medal 1986/87 (with Liverpool)
FA Cup winner's medal 1990/91 (with Tottenham Hotspur)
FA Charity Shield medal 1991* (with Tottenham Hotspur)
   *Trophy shared

Paul Walsh was signed as an apprentice for Charlton in October 1977 and progressed through the Club's youth system to sign as a professional in October 1979.

He made his first team debut during the disastrous 1979/80 season, playing in nine matches, and he was then paired up front with Derek Hales for 1980/81 as the Addicks gained promotion from the Third Division at the first attempt. His total of 18 goals only being eclipsed by his mentor, Hales, with 23. It was evident, even in those early days, that Charlton had unearthed another supremely talented striker.

It did not take the young forward long to make his mark back in the Second Division in 1981/82. In September he was on target in the second League match, hitting the second goal in the 2-0 home win against Blackburn Rovers, and he followed that up with a brace in another 2-0 home victory over Grimsby Town. He scored twice in the next fixture too, at Chelsea, in a 2-2 draw.

In October he netted another brace in SE7 as his two early strikes saw off Sheffield Wednesday 3-0, and November saw him add one more to his total at home to Leicester City, but this time it was in a painful 1-4 defeat.

He then missed a few matches through injury but by the turn of the year he had eight goals to his name.

He and his partner in crime, Hales, both scored at Grimsby Town in January in a lively 3-3 draw, and he netted again the following week at home in the local derby with Crystal Palace, where the Addicks edged through 2-1.

The convincing 5-2 home victory over Orient in March saw Walsh net the second Addicks' goal and he then added two more goals to his total during April.

He put the Addicks ahead at Rotherham United only for the Millers to hit back with two late goals to inflict a 1-2 defeat, and in the only victory in the last 11 matches, it was Walsh who netted the decisive goal in the 1-0 Valley win against Bolton Wanderers.

That brought his total to 13 goals for the season and he was the Club's top scorer in the League as Hales' total of 13 included two cup goals.

So having scored 31 goals in two seasons, Walsh was in demand. Luton Town, having won the Second Division Championship, offered Charlton a deal worth £350,000 (£250,000 plus striker Steve White, valued at £100,000) (=£1.2m) for the young talent and Walsh was on his way to Kenilworth Road and First Division football in July 1982.

He went on to enjoy a magnificent career, winning England U21 and Full caps while at Luton and was voted Young Player of the Year in 1984.

In May 1984, Liverpool paid £700,000 (=£2.2m) to take Walsh to Anfield where he helped the Reds win the First Division Championship in 1986. After four successful years on Merseyside, Walsh returned to London to sign for Tottenham Hotspur for a fee of £550,000 (=£1.5m) and he helped them to win the FA Cup in 1991.

He had a brief loan spell at Queens Park Rangers in September 1991 and eventually moved to Portsmouth in June 1992 for £400,000 (=£834,000). He featured in the "First Match Back at the Valley" in December 1992, coming on as substitute for Pompey as his namesake, Colin Walsh, scored that memorable goal to secure the Addicks a 1-0 win on their return to their spiritual home.

March 1994 saw him on the move again, this time to Manchester City who paid £750,000 (=£1.5m) to take him back north where he played at the top level again, this time in the Premier League.

He returned to Portsmouth in September 1995 when they paid a fee of £600,000 (=£1.1m) and he finished his career at Fratton Park, retiring due to a cruciate ligament injury in February 1996.

His career spanned 521 Football/Premier League games during which he netted 128 goals.

After retirement, Paul carved out a career in the media, becoming a regular pundit on Sky Sports football coverage.

Charlton Career:

Seasons: 1979/80 – 1981/82

Football League: 85+2A 24G

FA Cup: 4A 1G

League Cup: 9A 6G

Total: 98+2A 31G

1982/83   Derek Hales

Football League – Second Division

Leading Scorer: Derek Hales

Football League:	30A	14G
FA Cup:	1A	1G
League Cup:	<u>2A</u>	<u>2G</u>
Total	33A	17G

Season 1982/83 saw a number of changes at The Valley. In June 1982, Chairman and owner Michael Gliksten sold the Club to Mark Hulyer, thus ending the Gliksten family's 50 year ownership of Charlton Athletic.

Then, Manager Alan Mullery resigned, stating that he wouldn't work with Hulyer. Assistant Manager, Ken Craggs, replaced Mullery.

The only constant amongst all this change was the presence of Derek Hales who continued to provide his usual quota of goals.

With young star, Paul Walsh, now departed, Hales had a new strike partner in Steve White who had arrived from Luton Town as part of the Walsh deal. White was a proven goal scorer at Bristol Rovers and Luton so expectations were high that he and Hales would form a productive partnership.

The season opened with a promising 2-1 win at Leicester City but then things started to unravel with four successive defeats. The rot was stopped at Oldham Athletic where the Addicks came away with a point in a 2-2 draw with Hales on target. He scored in the next match too, at home to Fulham, who were dispatched 3-0.

October saw him on target at Carlisle United in a 1-4 defeat and he also scored in another away loss, at Chelsea, which finished 1-3.

In the League Cup second round, Charlton lost the first leg 0-3 to Luton Town at Kenilworth Road. Two goals from Hales, one a penalty, in the second leg gave the Addicks a 2-0 win but the Hatters, with Paul Walsh playing up front, went through on aggregate.

November saw the arrival of another striker, Allan Simonsen from Barcelona. Quite how Mark Hulyer managed to lure the former European Footballer of the Year to The Valley remains a mystery, but there he was and he made his debut in the home match with Middlesbrough. Charlton were 0-3 down at the interval but late goals from Hales and Simonsen almost earned them an unlikely point in a 2-3 defeat.

The next home game against Rotherham United proved to be even worse.

Despite Hales giving the hosts the lead, they ultimately slumped to a 1-5 defeat. Ken Craggs paid the ultimate price and was sacked. The team had only won five League games in three months so the latest debacle was the proverbial final straw. Reserve Team Coach, Lennie Lawrence, was put in temporary charge.

December brought two welcome home wins, against Newcastle United (2-0) with Simonsen on target, and Barnsley (3-2) with Hales netting a brace after Simonsen's opener.

Hales had netted ten goals by the end of the year and had been ably supported by White with seven. Lennie Lawrence lost his "caretaker" title in December and was appointed Manager.

Hales' next goal came in the FA Cup third round at The Valley in January. The visitors were First Division high flyers, Ipswich Town, but early goals by Martin Robinson and Hales gave the Addicks a 2-0 lead and an upset was on the cards. It was not to be however, as the Tractor Boys fought back to level things at 2-2 and then scored in the last minute to cruelly eliminate the hosts 2-3.

In February, Hales hit a last minute winner against Cambridge United in SE7 to secure a 2-1 victory, after Simonsen had scored the equaliser from the penalty spot.

However, at the end of the month there was another debacle. The visit to Turf Moor to play Burnley turned out to be a horror show. Hales did score but the Addicks were taken apart 1-7 and finished the match with nine men. Hales and Mark Aizlewood were both sent off when the score was 1-2 and the hosts ran riot, scoring five late goals.

A suspension followed and Hales' next goal did not arrive until April when his early strike at The Valley led to the 4-1 defeat of Oldham Athletic.

The Addicks were still fighting for survival and in the penultimate home match against Wolverhampton Wanderers in May, they found themselves 0-3 down at half-time. An incredible fight back in the second-half saw the hosts pull back to 2-3 before Hales grabbed the vital equaliser to secure a 3-3 draw.

However, everything rested on the last match of the season at home Bolton Wanderers. Both sides needed a victory to ensure they stayed up. Bolton took the lead after an hour and things looked bleak, until Hales turned the game on its head. He scored twice, the second a penalty after he had been brought down, and further goals from Steve Gritt and Carl Harris clinched a 4-1 win and survival. Bolton were relegated instead.

So it was another close call as the Addicks finished in 17th position and avoided relegation by three points.

Steve White enjoyed a good season, netting 12 times, but Hales finished as top scorer, for the sixth time, with 17 goals which brought his grand total up to 149.

Charlton Career:

See Season 1984/85

1983/84   Derek Hales

Football League – Second Division

Leading Scorer: Derek Hales

Football League: 27+2A   10G

FA Cup: 1A   0G

League Cup: 2A   1G

                Total   30+2A   11G

For the 1983/84 season, a new strike partner had to be found for Derek Hales as Steve White had been sold to Bristol Rovers during the close season.

So Hales started the season alongside Chris Jones, who had joined from Crystal Palace, before Ronnie Moore was signed from Rotherham United in September and became his more regular partner up front.

Charlton started the campaign in good form and were undefeated in the opening seven League matches. During that spell Hales was on target in the home matches against Carlisle United, scoring the only goal in a 1-0 win, and against Sheffield Wednesday when he netted a penalty in a 1-1 draw.

He scored for a third consecutive home game in the League Cup second round (second leg) against Brentford. The Addicks were 0-3 down from the first leg so although Hales scored in the 2-1 win it was the West Londoners who went through on aggregate.

The promising start to the season came to a shuddering halt in October. The visit to Brighton & Hove Albion ended in an eye-watering 0-7 defeat with the Addicks "lucky to get nil" following an abject performance.

Following that chastening score-line, results did gradually improve later in the month and Hales was again on target in consecutive home matches. He netted the decisive goal in a 1-0 victory over Manchester City, and he then converted a penalty against Swansea City as the Addicks came back from 0-2 down to draw 2-2.

He hit a lean spell in November and then missed five matches though injury but returned to fitness just after Christmas. In his first game back he scored the winner in a 1-0 Valley victory over Crystal Palace and he was on target in the next match too at home to Huddersfield Town. However, his equaliser proved to be in vain as the Terriers inflicted a 1-2 defeat.

The home match with Cambridge United in January was significant for two reasons. Firstly, Hales scored a brace, including a penalty, in the emphatic 5-2 victory, and secondly it marked the return to the Club of Hales' former strike partner, Mike Flanagan, from Queens Park Rangers. Flanagan played a wider role, in support of Hales and Moore, but it was good to see the pair back on the pitch together and with their previous differences resolved.

At this time the Club were in serious financial difficulties and were facing a winding-up order from the Inland Revenue. The Club was only saved on the 8th March when a rescue package from the Sunley Group was accepted by the High Court.

The next match following this drama was fittingly at The Valley. Grimsby Town were the visitors and it was Hales who scored the opening goal of the game. A young Robert Lee, who was making his League debut alongside Hales, netted the second goal to give the Addicks a 2-0 lead. But Grimsby had not read the script, and the final score was 3-3 with the Mariners scoring in the last minute after Martin Robinson had seemingly grabbed a late winner for the hosts.

Although a victory would have been a fitting way to celebrate the Club's survival and to welcome the new owners, nothing could quell the fans' joy and relief at their club still being in existence.

Back to the football and Hales netted his final goal of the season two matches later when he scored the equaliser at Blackburn Rovers in a 1-1 draw.

He did not play in the last nine matches of the season through injury and he was certainly missed as seven of them were defeats, including the last five.

Charlton finished mid-table in 13th position which, given all the off-field problems, was pretty respectable. Hales was top scorer, for a seventh time, with 11 goals bringing his grand total to 160. Stuart Leary's record of 163 was now tantalisingly in sight.

If there was any doubt that Hales could break the record, they were soon dispelled in the opening match of the 1984/85 campaign. Charlton were away to Cardiff City in the first League match and came away with the points following a 3-0 victory. Hales netted a hat-trick, with one coming from a penalty, to equal Leary's record. Three days later he broke the record at The Valley against Huddersfield Town. The Addicks recovered from a 0-2 deficit to draw 2-2 with Hales scoring goal number 164 in the process. For good measure he netted number 165 in the next match four days later, again at The Valley, as Notts County were defeated 3-0.

Hales was now 33 and in the twilight of his career. He struggled with injuries and was unable to maintain a regular place in the starting line-up where Robert Lee was now establishing himself as the heir to Hales' throne.

In March 1985 he left the Club to sign for Gillingham. He had made 16 appearances (14+2A) up to that point and scored 8 goals, to maintain his excellent strike rate.

He had, therefore, set a new Club record of **168 goals** in all competitions, surpassing Leary's record of 163 which had stood since 1962. Leary still held the record for League goals (153), compared to Hales' 148, but Hales had netted 20 cup goals to eclipse Leary's 10.

Derek played for Gillingham until 1986 when he retired at the age of 34. He is still Charlton's record goal scorer in all competitions and his total of 168 is unlikely ever to be beaten.

In 2012, The Charlton Athletic Museum established the Club's **Hall of Fame**. Three players are inducted into it each year following a vote by the supporters. It was no surprise that Derek Hales was among the first inductees, along with Sam Bartram and Clive Mendonca.

Charlton Career:

Seasons: 1973/74 – 1976/77, 1978/79 – 1984/85

Football League: 312+8A 148G

FA Cup: 17A 5G

League Cup: 31A 15G

Total: 360+8A 168G

1984/85   Mike Flanagan

Football League – Second Division

Leading Scorer: Mike Flanagan

Football League:	38A	11G
FA Cup:	2A	0G
League Cup:	<u>2A</u>	<u>0G</u>
Total	42A	11G

Mike Flanagan
CHARLTON ATHLETIC FC

Mike Flanagan had returned to Charlton from Queens Park Rangers in January 1984, with the Addicks paying a fee of £50,000 (=£162,000).

For season 1984/85, Flanagan was deployed in a wide role by Lennie Lawrence, supporting strikers Hales and Lee. He netted his first goal of the campaign in September at Grimsby Town but the Addicks lost 1-2 in what was their first League defeat.

He was on target later in the month at Wimbledon where the Addicks triumphed 3-1, and his third strike came back in SE7 in October in a 1-2 defeat to Fulham. That goal was his 100th for the Club.

In November he hit the equaliser at Sheffield United to earn a 1-1 draw but he had to wait until February to hit his fifth goal of the season. It was a significant strike as it clinched a 1-0 win at Fratton Park against Portsmouth.

March opened with a Valley goal-fest, Barnsley being seen off 5-3 as the Addicks came back from a 0-3 deficit. Flanagan scored the decisive third goal to square things up at 3-3 and set up an unlikely victory.

Shortly after this, Hales left for Gillingham and Flanagan took on more of the striking responsibilities with Robert Lee. He responded by netting the winner as the Addicks edged past Wolverhampton Wanderers 1-0 at The Valley.

He replicated the feat in the next home match which also finished 1-0, this time against Middlesbrough, and in the final fixtures of the campaign he netted three times. First he scored at Birmingham City in a 1-2 reverse, then in the final home game against Oxford United he hit a brace in a 3-3 draw.

Charlton finished in a disappointing 17th position but Flanagan topped the scoring charts with 11 goals. Robert Lee was close behind him with 10.

Flanagan's grand total for Charlton now stood at 108 goals.

The following season 1985/86, proved to be his last at the Club but he went out in a blaze of glory. In a campaign which ended with a return to the First Division for the first time in 29 years, Flanagan played a significant part.

He hit 12 goals, finishing as the third highest scorer, and took his grand total to 120 in all competitions. That put him in third place behind Hales and Leary in the Club's all-time goal scoring list, a position that he still retains.

In August 1986 he moved to Cambridge United and spent one last season in the Football League before retiring in 1987 aged 34.

He did return to Charlton in October 1987 to work as a coach under Lennie Lawrence, but he left in August 1990 following a disagreement with the manager.

He then had a spell with Margate as a player before venturing into management with Gillingham (1993-95), Waterford United in Ireland, Margate as assistant manager, Malden & Tiptree and Brentwood Town.

Mike Flanagan gave great service to the Addicks, over two spells, and his 120 goals confirm him as one of the Club's greatest strikers. This was recognised in 2020 when he was inducted into Charlton's Hall of Fame.

Charlton Career:

Seasons: 1971/72 – 1978/79, 1983/84 – 1985/86

Football League: 330+17A 109G

FA Cup: 20+1A 3G

League Cup: 27A 8G

Full Members Cup: 1A 0G

Total: 378+18A 120G

1985/86 John Pearson

Football League – Second Division

Leading Scorer: John Pearson

Football League: 42A 14G

FA Cup: 1A   0G

League Cup: 2A   0G

Full Members Cup: <u>2A   1G</u>

Total   47A 15G

John Stuart Pearson

Born: Sheffield, 1.9.1963

Career:
Sheffield Wednesday (FL 64+41A 24G)
Charlton Athletic (FL 52+9A 15G)
Leeds United (FL 51+48A 12G)
Rotherham United (loan) (FL 11A 5G)
Barnsley (FL 29+3A 4G)
Hull City (loan) (FL 15A 0G)
Carlisle United (FL 5+3A 0G)
Mansfield Town (FL 0+2A 0G)
Cardiff City (FL 12A 0G)
Merthyr Tydfil

Honours:
England Youth
Second Division runners-up 1983/84 (with Sheffield Wednesday)
Second Division runners-up 1985/86 (with Charlton Athletic)
Second Division Championship medal 1989/90 (with Leeds United)

John Pearson started his career with his local club, Sheffield Wednesday, signing as an apprentice in June 1979 and as a professional May 1981.

He scored on his League debut and in 1984 helped the Owls gain promotion to the First Division by clinching the runners-up spot in the Second Division. He had played in 105 League matches for the Owls before moving to Charlton in May 1985.

During the 1985/86 close season, Lennie Lawrence made six signings for Charlton as he assembled a squad capable of challenging for promotion. Pearson was one of them and he became a key component in the squad, the 6ft 2in centre-forward bringing aerial power and goals. The fee of £100,000 (=£305,000) proved to be money well spent.

He scored on his Addicks' debut in the first match of the season, netting the second goal to defeat Barnsley 2-1 at The Valley. He was on target in the second match too when he hit the equaliser to secure a point in a 2-2 draw at Grimsby Town.

In September he scored against Crystal Palace in a 3-1 home win, but Charlton's good form was marred by the announcement at that match that the Addicks would be vacating The Valley to groundshare with their visitors at Selhurst Park. Two weeks later, Charlton played their last game in SE7 against Stoke City where a 2-0 win was almost irrelevant amongst the protests and despair of the home supporters.

So Selhurst Park became Charlton's 'home' ground for the rest of the season and even longer as it turned out. Pearson scored his first goal there in a Full Members Cup tie against Chelsea which ended in a 1-3 defeat. A week later he scored his first League goal at the new home venue as Shrewsbury Town were dispatched 4-1.

Another home win, against Carlisle United, at the end of November saw Pearson open the scoring in 3-0 victory and he did the same against visitors Grimsby Town, just prior to Christmas, in a 2-0 triumph.

In January, Leeds United were dismantled 4-0 at Selhurst with Pearson netting his eighth goal of the season. That started a run of 19 matches, in which only two were lost, as the Addicks closed in on promotion.

Pearson scored in one of those defeats, at home to Portsmouth (1-2), and also in the next match at Bradford City where the Addicks triumphed 2-1.

Then there came another new signing, striker Jim Melrose from Manchester City, in a bid to boost the push for promotion. He was paired up front with Pearson who, up to that point, had been partnered by Robert Lee.

Pearson scored the decisive goal in the 1-0 home victory over eventual champions Norwich City, and he scored in the next home match too. Huddersfield Town were beaten 3-0 with goals from Melrose (2) and Pearson.

At the end of April, Charlton won three consecutive matches and Pearson was on target in all of them. It started at Fulham (3-0), home to Blackburn Rovers (3-0) and at home to Fulham (2-0). That brought his total for the season to 15 goals.

May dawned and there were still two matches to play. A memorable visit to Carlisle United saw the Addicks fight back from 0-2 down to win 3-2 and clinch promotion back to the First Division for the first time for 29 years.

The final match at Selhurst was against fellow promotion rivals Wimbledon and ended 0-0, a result which ultimately confirmed Charlton as runners-up with Wimbledon also gaining promotion in third place.

John Pearson had certainly repaid his transfer fee. He played in all 47 League and cup matches and finished as top scorer with 15 goals. He was ably supported by Mark Stuart (13) and Mike Flanagan (12). Melrose also made an impact during his late season cameo, scoring five times in only 11 appearances.

For the 1986/87 First Division campaign, Pearson continued to lead the Charlton attack but, as the season progressed, he lost his place to Melrose and eventually left the Club in January 1987. Leeds United, then of the Second Division, paid a fee of £72,000 (=£204,000) to take the big striker back to Yorkshire.

Ironically, Charlton would meet Leeds in the Play-off final at the end of season and Pearson would line-up against his old club. Charlton won that particular battle to retain their top flight status, but Leeds would win the Second Division Championship in 1990 with Pearson in their ranks.

In 1991, he had a loan spell at Rotherham United and then signed for Barnsley later that year. He also had spells with Hull City, Carlisle United, and Mansfield Town. His last League club was Cardiff City, who he joined in

January 1995, before winding down his senior career with Merthyr Tydfil in the Southern League.

John Pearson's Football League career spanned 345 matches and he scored 60 goals. He is now back at Hillsborough working for the Sheffield Wednesday Community Programme.

He will always be remembered at Charlton for being a key member of the squad which delivered First Division football back to the Club.

Charlton Career:

Seasons: 1985/56 – 1986/87

Football League: 52+9A 15G

FA Cup: 1A 0G

League Cup: 3+3A 0G

Full Members Cup: 4A 1G

Total: 60+12A 16G

1986/87   Jim Melrose

Football League – First Division

Leading Scorer: Jim Melrose

Football League: 30+4A   14G

FA Cup: 1A   0G

League Cup: 4A   0G

Full Members Cup: 3+1A   0G

Play-Offs: <u>5A   3G</u>

Total   43+5A   17G

James Millsop Melrose

Born: Glasgow, 7.10.1958

Career:
Eastercraigs FC
Partick Thistle (SL 103+19A 31G)
Leicester City (FL 57+15A 21G)
Coventry City (FL 21+3A 8G)
Celtic (SL 20+10A 7G)
Wolverhampton Wanderers (loan) (FL 6+1A 2G)
Manchester City (FL 27+7A 8G)
Charlton Athletic (FL 44+4A 19G)
Leeds United (FL 3+1A 0G)
Shrewsbury Town (FL 27+22A 3G)
Macclesfield Town
Curzon Ashton
Halesowen Harriers

Honours:
Scotland Schools
Scotland U21 – 8 caps (with Partick Thistle)
Scottish League v Irish League 1980 (with Partick Thistle)
Scottish League Cup runners-up medal 1984 (with Celtic)
Scottish FA Cup runners-up medal 1984 (with Celtic)
FL Second Division runners-up 1985/86 (with Charlton)
Full Members Cup runners-up medal 1987 (with Charlton)

Jim Melrose made his name with Partick Thistle, signing for them as a part-time professional in 1975. He did well for the Jags and also represented the Scottish League and was capped by Scotland at Under-21 level.

In July 1980 he was signed by Leicester City, who had just won promotion to the First Division, for a fee of £250,000 (=£1m). He moved on to Coventry City, in exchange for Tom English, in September 1982 but returned to Scotland a year later to join Celtic in a £100,000 (=£355,000) deal.

He had a loan spell with Wolverhampton Wanderers in September 1984 and two months later made a permanent move to Manchester City who paid a fee of £40,000 (=£90,000). He helped City win promotion to the First Division in 1985 when they clinched the third promotion spot in the Second Division.

Lennie Lawrence signed him for Charlton in March 1986 to provide the final impetus in their battle for promotion. The fee of £45,000 (=£133,000) was another shrewd investment. His five goals in only 11 appearances helped to clinch the runners-up spot and promotion to the First Division.

In the top flight for 1986/87, Melrose proved pivotal in maintaining the Addicks' First Division status.

He actually began the season on the substitutes bench and did not make his first start until mid-September, at Liverpool, in a 0-2 defeat. His first goal arrived two matches later, when he scored in the 2-3 loss at Oxford United.

In October he produced a stellar performance at Selhurst Park against, eventual champions, Everton. The Addicks gained only their third win of the season as Melrose netted a memorable hat-trick to secure a 3-2 victory.

Two weeks later he set a new Club record by scoring after only 9 seconds at Upton Park against West Ham United. It was the fastest recorded goal in Charlton's history. The Addicks also took all the points in a 3-1 win.

Having won four games in a row, Charlton went into free-fall and failed to register a win in the next nine matches. That dismal run came to an end in emphatic style just after Christmas when Manchester City were routed

5-0 at Selhurst with Melrose providing the third goal.

Then came another dismal run of seven matches without a victory during January and February, although Melrose did get on the scoresheet twice. First at Sheffield Wednesday in a 1-1 draw and then at Coventry City in a 1-2 defeat.

The sequence was broken in March when Melrose hit a brace to defeat West Ham United 2-1 at Selhurst. He then hit an equaliser at Everton but the Addicks conceded a late goal to go down 1-2.

His next goal came in April in a seven goal thriller at Selhurst Park. Watford were the visitors and with the Addicks leading 3-1 at one point, the Hornets hit back to level at 3-3, only for Melrose to strike the winner to secure a 4-3 victory.

With Charlton still fighting for First Division survival, Melrose scored in two successive matches at the end of the month. He notched the third goal in the 3-0 home victory over Aston Villa and then scored at The Dell against Southampton which eventually finished 2-2.

The Addicks won their last two games in May to secure 19th position which would normally guarantee survival. Ironically two of Melrose's former clubs, Leicester City and Manchester City, finished below the Addicks and were relegated along with Aston Villa.

However, this was the first season of the Play-off system and Charlton had to play off against the teams finishing third, fourth and fifth in the Second Division to retain their First Division status.

Melrose already had 14 League goals to his name but he was to significantly add to that total in the Play-offs.

Charlton had to play Ipswich Town in the two-leg semi-final. The first match at Portman Road ended 0-0 but in the second-leg at Selhurst Park, Melrose scored twice as Ipswich were edged out 2-1.

The two-leg Final was against Leeds United with the first-leg being played in South London. In a tight game, Melrose scored three minutes from full-time to give the Addicks a priceless 1-0 lead in the tie. Two days later, Leeds came back to win 1-0 at Elland Road so the Final had to go to a replay.

Birmingham City's St Andrews was selected as the neutral venue so five days later the teams met again. It was another tight encounter which ended 0-0 after 90 minutes but the real drama was to come in extra-time.

Nine minutes in, John Sheridan scored for Leeds with a free-kick and the Addicks looked doomed. With only seven minutes remaining, defender Peter Shirtliff hit Charlton's equaliser and, amazingly, four minutes later the same player netted the winner ! Charlton were staying up.

Jim Melrose ended the season as top scorer with 17 goals, with the three in the Play-offs proving priceless.

It was somehow ironic then that Melrose joined Leeds United just five months later. After playing in only three matches the following season, Leeds paid £50,000 (=£140,000) to take him back north. His home was in Manchester so the move made sense for him, although the Charlton fans were dismayed to see him go.

The move to Elland Road did not really work out for him and he joined Shrewsbury Town, initially on loan in February 1988, before signing permanently a month later. The Shrews paid another £50,000 (=£135,000) fee and he stayed at Gay Meadow until 1990. He wound down his senior career in non-league football with Macclesfield Town, Curzon Ashton and Halesowen Harriers.

His Football League and Scottish League career totaled 390 matches, 99 goals, and nine clubs.

His contribution to Charlton's cause should not be underestimated. His five goals were instrumental in getting the Addicks back into the First Division and his 17 goals the following season most certainly enabled them to stay there.

Charlton Career:

Seasons: 1985/86 – 1987/88

Football League: 44+4A 19G

FA Cup: 1A 0G

League Cup: 4A 0G

Full Members Cup: 3+1A 0G

Play-Offs: 5A 3G

Total: 57+5A 22G

1987/88   Garth Crooks

Football League – First Division

Leading Scorer: Garth Crooks

Football League:	24+4A	10G
FA Cup:	0+1A	0G
League Cup:	2A	2G
Full Members Cup:	1A	0G
Total	27+5A	12G

Garth Anthony Crooks

Born: Bucknall, Stoke-on-Trent, 10.3.1958

Career:
Stoke City (FL 141+6A 48G)
Tottenham Hotspur (FL 121+4A 48G)
Manchester United (loan) (FL 6+1A 2G)
West Bromwich Albion (FL 39+1A 16G)
Charlton Athletic (FL 41+15A 15G)

Honours:
England U21 – 4 caps – 3 Goals (with Stoke City)
FA Cup winners' medal 1981 (with Tottenham Hotspur)
FA Cup winners' medal 1982 (with Tottenham Hotspur)
UEFA Cup winners' medal 1984 (with Tottenham Hotspur)
Football League Cup runners-up medal 1982 (with Tottenham Hotspur)

Garth Crooks joined his home town club, Stoke City, as an apprentice in 1974 and was signed as a professional in March 1976.

He developed into a pacey forward and a natural finisher and was instrumental in Stoke regaining their First Division status in 1979 by clinching the third promotion place in the Second Division. Having netted 48 League goals for Stoke, he was involved in a big money move to Tottenham Hotspur in July 1980, with Spurs paying a fee of £600,000 (=£2.6m).

He spent five years at White Hart Lane, where he developed a lethal partnership with Steve Archibald, and helped Spurs to win two FA Cups and the UEFA Cup. In November 1983 he had a loan spell at Manchester United before joining West Bromwich Albion in August 1985 for £100,000 (=£305,000).

He arrived at Charlton in March 1987, in exchange for a £75,000

(=£212,000), fee and helped the Addicks maintain their First Division status, via the Play-offs, in 1986/87.

The departure of Jim Melrose early in 1987/88 meant that Crooks had a number of strike partners during the campaign, Mark Stuart, Robert Lee, Paul Williams, Carl Leaburn and, new signing, Andy Jones.

Charlton opened the season with four defeats before getting a point at Portsmouth in a 1-1 draw. Crooks opened his goal-scoring account in the next fixture, at Anfield, where the Addicks went down 2-3 to Liverpool despite twice taking the lead.

The long awaited first win came in the next match at home Luton Town and it was Crooks who secured it by netting the only goal in a 1-0 victory. He scored for the third consecutive match in the League Cup second round (first leg) at Selhurst Park against Walsall. Crooks hit two late goals in a 3-0 win.

In October he found the net at West Ham United in a 1-1 draw but from the end of the month, he missed nine matches through injury before returning to the substitute's bench in January. At the half way point of the season, the Addicks had only recorded three League wins and were deep in the relegation mire. Crooks was eventually restored to the starting line-up in February against Sheffield Wednesday at Selhurst. He scored a brace in a much needed 3-0 win.

In March he scored in two successive victories. First he netted a brace at home to West Ham United (3-0) and he then scored at Southampton where the Addicks secured a rare away win (1-0).

From the beginning of March, Charlton's form had improved dramatically, in fact in the last 11 matches of the season they lost only once. Crooks hit another brace during that run when he got both goals in the 2-0 home win against Newcastle United. Following that victory, the last three matches were all drawn 1-1, including the last match at Stamford Bridge where the point secured the Addicks' survival and sent Chelsea into the Play-offs.

Charlton finished in 17th position which, given their early season form, was a minor miracle. Garth Crooks finished as top scorer with 12 goals and was the only Charlton player to reach double figures.

He stayed with Charlton for another two years but was hampered by a persistent back injury with restricted his appearances to only 27 matches, in which he scored four goals. He finally announced his retirement in November 1990 at the age of 32.

He had enjoyed a magnificent career and his League matches alone amounted to 375 appearances, in which he scored 129 goals. He was, of course, at the peak of his powers at Tottenham and when he came to Charlton he was in the twilight of his career. It was nevertheless a pleasure to see a player of his undoubted class pull on the red jersey.

Crooks was always an eloquent speaker, and had been chairman of the PFA during his career, so it was a natural progression that he should become one of the leading football pundits for BBC Sport. In 1999 he was awarded the OBE in recognition of his services in that role.

Charlton Career:

Seasons: 1986/87 – 1990/91

Football League: 41+15A 15G

FA Cup: 3+1A 1G

League Cup: 3+1A 2G

Full Members Cup: 2A 0G

Play-Offs: 5A 0G

Total: 54+17A 18G

1988/89   Paul Williams

Football League – First Division

Leading Scorer: Paul Williams

Football League:	30+2A	13G
FA Cup:	3A	2G
League Cup:	3A	2G
Total	36+2A	17G

Paul Williams
CHARLTON ATHLETIC FC

Paul Anthony Williams

Born: Stratford, London, 16.8.1965

Career:
Aveley
Clapton
Woodford Town
Charlton Athletic (FL 74+8A 23G)
Brentford (loan) (FL 7A 3G)
Sheffield Wednesday (FL 78+15A 25G)
Crystal Palace (FL/PL 38+8A 7G)
Sunderland (loan) (FL 3A 0G)
Birmingham City (loan) (FL 8+3A 0G)
Charlton Athletic (FL 2+7A 0G)
Torquay United (loan) (FL 9A 0G)
Southend United (FL 30+9A 7G)
Canvey Island
Bowers FC

Honours:
England U21 – 4 caps – 3 goals (with Charlton)
England 'B' – 3 caps (with Charlton)
Football League Cup winners' medal 1990/91 (with Sheffield Wed)
First Division*Championship medal 1993/94 (with Crystal Palace)
(*Tier 2)

Following a number of unsuccessful trials with London League clubs, Paul Williams plied his trade in non-league football until Charlton spotted him playing for Woodford Town.

After a brief trial, he was given a chance to fulfill his potential, at the age of 21, and was signed as a professional in August 1986. Woodford Town received compensation in the form of a fee of £12,000 (=£35,000).

He made his First Division debut at Wimbledon a year later but did not establish himself as a first team regular with the Addicks until the 1988/89 campaign, which proved to be his breakthrough season.

He scored the first League goals of his career in the second match of the season at West Ham United, netting a brace in a 3-1 victory. Later in September he was on target in three successive matches starting with a goal against Newcastle United at Selhurst Park in a 2-2 draw. Then he hit the equaliser in the League Cup second round tie at Northampton Town which also finished all square (1-1), and finally he scored two goals at Norwich City in the League as the Addicks gained an impressive 3-1 win.

October brought two more goals for the pacey striker, both at home, against Aston Villa (2-2) and Sheffield Wednesday (2-1). The next match was in the League Cup third round at Queens Park Rangers where Williams gave the Addicks a 1-0 lead at the interval. However, Rangers hit back in the second-half and scored twice to inflict a 1-2 defeat.

In November, Williams put Charlton ahead against Everton at Selhurst but again the Addicks couldn't hold the lead and went down 1-2. Shortly after this, he suffered an injury which caused him to miss five matches, only returning to the bench for the last match of the year, a home draw with West Ham United (0-0). By this time his goal tally stood at 10.

January was a particularly productive month for him as he scored in three games, all at Selhurst Park. It started in the FA Cup third round tie with Oldham Athletic when he netted a last minute winner to clinch a 2-1 victory. Back in the League he hit the net again in the 3-0 defeat of Luton Town, before scoring again in the FA Cup fourth round tie with non-league Kettering

Town, as the Addicks edged through 2-1.

Goal 14 arrived in February at White Hart Lane as the Addicks took a point in a 1-1 draw, and in March he scored in successive matches, at Sheffield Wednesday in a 1-3 defeat and at home to Southampton in a 2-2 draw.

His final goal of the season came in the last home match in May. The Addicks beat Derby County 3-0 at Selhurst Park to secure First Division football for another season and Williams had the privilege of slotting the third goal past Peter Shilton.

Charlton finished in 14th position and Paul Williams was top scorer with 17 goals, 13 of them in the League.

He had proved that he possessed the ability to play at the top level and he was rewarded in June by being included in the England U21 squad for the tournament in Toulon, in which he won four caps and netted three goals.

He was turning out to be quite a find.

Charlton Career:

See Season 1989/90

1989/90   Paul Williams

Football League – First Division

Leading Scorer: Paul Williams

Football League: 38A 10G

FA Cup: 3A   1G

League Cup: 3A   1G

Total   44A 12G

Charlton made a promising start to their fourth season back at the top level.

The first three matches were all drawn which included the match at The Den against Millwall which finished 2-2. Not a bad result on the face of it but when Williams scored the Addicks' second goal with only five minutes to go it looked like a certain away win. The Lions somehow scored twice in the final minutes to level things up at 2-2.

The fourth fixture was also a London derby with Chelsea visiting Selhurst. Two goals from Williams wrapped up a comprehensive 3-0 victory.

However, there was then a dramatic loss of form. The next four matches were all lost and the Addicks failed to score in any of them. There was some respite in the League Cup second round (2nd leg) at Hereford United. Leading 3-1 from the 1st leg, Williams scored the only goal to secure a 1-0 win and send the Addicks through 4-1 on aggregate.

Back in the League, he was on target in the next match too, at home to Tottenham Hotspur, when he gave the Addicks the lead in the second-half. But three late goals from Spurs made it 1-3, inflicting a fifth successive League defeat.

The poor run was arrested the following week with a welcome 1-0 win at Queens Park Rangers, then a point was gained at Coventry City in a 1-1 draw. Perhaps the best result of the season came in the next match, at home to Manchester United. A brace of goals from Williams secured a 2-0 victory and the hope that a corner had been turned.

Alas it hadn't. The next 12 League matches yielded only three points in a disastrous run of nine defeats and three draws. Williams was on target during this period against Manchester City at home in November (1-1), at Chelsea in January (1-3), and at Everton in February (1-2). He also scored in the FA Cup in January at Bradford City in a third round replay which finished 3-0 to the Addicks.

As the Addicks struggled, William's star was still rising and he won three England 'B' caps during the season.

The winless streak in the League was arrested in February with successive wins at home to Luton Town (2-0) and at Manchester City (2-1) followed by a 0-0 draw at Arsenal. But they were followed by two defeats before a William's goal earned a home point against Nottingham Forest (1-1) in March. That was his last goal of the season and proved to be his last goal for the Club.

Following the Forest draw, two more wins were recorded at Coventry City (2-1) and at home to QPR (1-0), but it all had the feeling of being too little, too late.

The last six games all ended in defeat with the 1-2 home loss to Wimbledon, in the third match of that sequence, finally confirming the Addicks' relegation.

The lack of their own home ground and without sufficient resources to strengthen the team, their demise was almost inevitable. Lennie Lawrence had worked a miracle by keeping them in the First Division for four seasons against all the odds.

Charlton finished in 19th position, only Millwall were below them. They only managed seven League wins and were a massive 13 points from safety.

Paul Williams had another good season and finished as top scorer with 12 goals while playing in a struggling side. He was also ever-present in the League, playing in all 38 matches.

With relegation comes the realisation that you are going to lose your best players. So it was with Williams and he moved to Sheffield Wednesday in August 1990 for a fee of £600,000 (=£1.3m).

Ironically, the Owls had been relegated to the Second Division with Charlton, but, with Williams in their ranks, they won promotion the following season (1990/91) to bounce straight back to the First Division. They also won the League Cup by beating Manchester United 1-0 at Wembley.

Williams did well at Hillsborough and formed a good partnership with David

Hirst, however, he returned to London to sign for Crystal Palace in September 1992 in a swap deal which took Mark Bright in the opposite direction. He won a First Division* Championship (Tier 2) medal with Palace in 1993/94, before having loan spells at Sunderland and Birmingham City during 1995.

Later that year, he returned to Charlton, who were by now back at The Valley, and he played a further nine matches for the Addicks before going on loan to Torquay United in March 1996. Five months later he made a permanent move to Southend United which was to be his final League club. He retired in 1998.

Despite making a late start in the professional game, Paul Williams' career record in the Football League/Premier League was 299 matches and 65 goals.

After leaving Southend, he returned to the non-league scene in Essex as player/coach with Canvey Island and then, in 2002, with Bowers FC.

Paul continued his coaching career as an Academy coach at Charlton and Crystal Palace, before taking up a coaching appointment in Florida in 2012.

Charlton Career:

Seasons: 1987/88 – 1989/90, 1995/96

Football League: 76+15A 23G

FA Cup: 6+1A 3G

League Cup: 6A 3G

Total: 88+16A 29G

1990/91   Robert Lee

Football League – Second Division

Leading Scorer: Robert Lee

Football League:	43A 13G
FA Cup:	1A 0G
League Cup:	2A 0G
Total	46A 13G

Robert Martin Lee

Born: Plaistow, London, 1.2.1966

Career:
Hornchurch
Charlton Athletic (FL 274+24A 59G)
Newcastle United (FL/PL 292+11A 44G)
Derby County (FL/PL 47+1A 2G)
West Ham United (FL 12+4A 0G)
Oldham Athletic (FL 0A 0G)
Wycombe Wanderers (FL 34+4A 0G)

Honours:
Havering Boys
England U21 – 2 caps (with Charlton)
England 'B' – 1 cap (with Newcastle Utd)
England Full International – 21 caps- 2 goals (with Newcastle Utd)
Full Members Cup runners-up medal 1986/87 (with Charlton)
First Division*Championship medal 1992/93 (with Newcastle Utd)
Premier League runners-up 1995/96 (with Newcastle Utd)
Premier League runners-up 1996/97 (with Newcastle Utd)
(*Tier 2)

Robert Lee joined Charlton as an apprentice after being spotted playing in non-league football for Hornchurch. He was signed as a professional in July 1983 and made his League debut in March 1984 against Grimsby Town at The Valley and scored in a 3-3 draw.

A skillful, right-sided forward, he helped the Addicks achieve promotion to the First Division in 1986 and spent nine seasons at the Club, during which he won two England U21 caps. His best season from a goal-scoring perspective was 1990/91 when he finished as the Club's leading scorer.

With Charlton newly relegated to the Second Division they made an appalling start to the new campaign and lost their opening four matches. Lee did score in the second fixture, a 1-2 defeat at Bristol Rovers, but the Addicks did not register a win until the seventh game, at home to Barnsley, who they edged past 2-1 at the end of September.

They failed to win any of the following four matches, although Lee did find the net in the home match with Watford, but the Hornets struck back to inflict a 1-2 defeat.

October did bring the second win, at Newcastle United, where Lee scored in a welcome 3-1 victory. A week later he netted at Notts County to secure a point in a 2-2 draw.

In November/December he scored in four successive matches as the Addicks' form finally improved. The sequence started at Middlesbrough where he opened the scoring in a 2-1 win, then he hit the net at home to Oxford United (3-3). Portsmouth were next up at Selhurst and his early goal set up a 2-1 win before he scored the crucial goal at Bristol City to secure all the points in a 1-0 victory.

Just before Christmas he netted the winner at home to Hull City (2-1) to bring his goal tally at the end of the year to nine.

Charlton were undefeated in the League in January and Lee grabbed his 10th of the season in February when he scored a late equaliser at Oxford United in a 1-1 draw.

Charlton enjoyed a successful March, winning five of the seven matches. Lee was on target in the last of these, a 2-0 home victory over West Bromwich Albion. He then scored in the next two matches going into April, at Hull City (2-2) and at Selhurst against Ipswich Town (1-1).

That proved to be his last strike of the season as he finished with 13 goals, all in the League. He was also, deservedly, voted Player of the Year.

Charlton finished in 16th position which was respectable given their dismal opening to the campaign.

The last home game of the season against West Ham United, which finished 1-1, was the last match of the Club's controversial ground-sharing agreement at Selhurst Park, as preparations were being made to move back to The Valley.

Robert Lee had scored the last goal at the home ground back in 1985 but, as it turned out, he would be denied the privilege of repeating that feat in SE7.

Delays in the refurbishment of The Valley meant that Charlton entered into another ground-sharing agreement, this time with West Ham United at Upton Park. It was there that they kicked off the 1991/92 season.

By this time, Manager Lennie Lawrence had left in July 1991 to join Middlesbrough, and he had been replaced by a joint-management team of Alan Curbishley and Steve Gritt, both senior players at the Club.

The 1991/92 campaign kicked off at Upton Park and Lee scored the Addicks' first goal at the new venue in a 2-1 victory over Newcastle United. He enjoyed another successful season, scoring 12 goals, and was attracting attention from other clubs.

In September 1992, Charlton cashed in on their talented striker. Newcastle United, managed by Kevin Keegan, paid £700,000 (=£1.4m) to take Lee to the north-east. Both clubs benefitted from the deal, Charlton needed the money to complete the refurbishment of The Valley, and Newcastle won the

First Division* Championship (Tier 2) at the end of the season to gain promotion to the Premier League.

Lee's career blossomed on Tyneside, with Newcastle twice finishing as runners-up in the Premier League, and he also gained international recognition, winning an England 'B' cap and 21 Full England caps.

After nearly ten successful years with the Magpies, Lee moved to Derby County in February 2002 for a fee of £250,000 (=£410,000). In August 2003 he moved on to West Ham United but only stayed for one season, moving briefly to Oldham Athletic November 2004.

He then signed for Wycombe Wanderers in March 2005 before finally retiring in 2006 at the age of 40.

He had enjoyed a magnificent career, appearing in 703 Football League/Premier League matches and netting 105 goals. His 343 appearances for Charlton is impressive enough but his transfer fee enabled the Club to return to The Valley, thus providing a lasting legacy.

Charlton Career:

Seasons: 1983/84 – 1992/93

Football League: 274+24A 59G

FA Cup: 14A 2G

League Cup: 16+3A 1G

Full Members Cup: 7+2A 3G

Anglo-Italian Cup: 1A 0G

Play-Offs: 2A 0G

Total: 314+29A 65G

1991/92   Carl Leaburn

Football League – Second Division

Leading Scorer: Carl Leaburn

Football League:	37+2A	11G
FA Cup:	3A	1G
League Cup:	<u>3A</u>	<u>2G</u>
Total	43+2A	14G

Carl Leaburn
CHARLTON ATHLETIC FC

Carl Winston Leaburn

Born: Lewisham, London, 30.3.1969

Career:
Charlton Athletic (FL 276+46A 53G)
Northampton Town (loan) (FL 9A 0G)
Wimbledon (PL/FL 36+23A 4G)
Queens Park Rangers (FL 0+1A 0G)
Grays Athletic

Honours:
FA Youth Cup runners-up medal 1986/87 (with Charlton)
England U20 Squad Member – Brazil Tour 1988 (with Charlton)

Carl Leaburn developed in Charlton's youth system and was signed as a professional in April 1987.

He was a member of the Addicks' successful Youth Team which reached the final of the FA Youth Cup that year, where they narrowly lost 1-2, on aggregate, to Coventry City.

He made his League debut, as a substitute, in the First Division match at Oxford United in March 1987, just days before his 18th birthday, and then made his first start a few weeks later at Newcastle United, when he scored in a 3-0 win.

A tall, rangy centre-forward, standing 6ft 3ins, Leaburn was an ideal target-man and, for a player of his size, he was as good with his feet as he was in the air. He had been a regular goal-scorer at youth and reserve level but he had trouble translating that ability into the rarefied atmosphere of League football.

Despite his lack of goals during his early seasons, he was still a valuable member of the team and set up many a goal for his strike partners, many of who were quick to acknowledge his selfless contribution.

In March 1990 he had a loan spell at Northampton Town, to gain more experience, but by the end of the 1990/91 season his 65(+26) appearances for the Addicks had yielded only 4 goals.

As the 1991/92 season kicked-off at the Addicks' temporary home venue of Upton Park, Leaburn was suddenly a different player. The first match against Newcastle United was won 2-1 with a confident looking Leaburn netting the second goal.

Three days later he was on target again, this time in the League Cup first round (1st leg) at home to Fulham, when he opened the scoring in a 4-2 victory. A week later, he scored in the second leg, which finished 1-1, to send the Addicks through 5-3 on aggregate.

The new management duo of Alan Curbishley and Steve Gritt had reshaped the team and Leaburn was partnered up front with the experienced Garry Nelson, signed from Brighton & Hove Albion. With Robert Lee operating on the right-wing and Colin Walsh on the left, Leaburn was thriving on the service he was receiving from both flanks.

His next strike came in September at home to Port Vale, Leaburn notched the second goal to add to Nelson's opener in a 2-0 victory. He then scored a couple of important goals in October, first netting the only goal of the game at home to Bristol Rovers (1-0), and then the equaliser at Southend United in a 1-1 draw which could have been so much better had the Addicks not contrived to miss, not one, but two penalties!

By Christmas, Leaburn's goal tally stood at six, hardly headline making stuff until you consider that he had only scored four times in the previous four years.

In the last match of the year, he grabbed another goal at Derby County in a 2-1 win, and he also scored in the next two games. Barnet were the visitors in the FA Cup third round and they were eventually seen off 3-1 with Leaburn netting the crucial second goal to put the Addicks ahead. Back in the League, he led the fightback at home to Oxford United as the Addicks came back from 0-2 to draw 2-2, with Leaburn and Lee saving the day.

In February, he scored the late, match-clinching, second goal at home to Southend United, who were dispatched 2-0, but his 11th goal of the season was only a consolation as the Addicks slumped to a home defeat at the hands of Grimsby Town (1-3).

Following that debacle, Charlton went on a ten match unbeaten run, winning six of them. Leaburn was on target in three matches during that spell, all coming away from home at - Swindon Town (2-1), Blackburn Rovers (2-0) and Portsmouth (2-1).

Following that successful run, the last two matches were both lost 0-1 and the Addicks narrowly missed out on the Play-offs by three points, finishing in 7th place. They had registered an amazing 11 away wins and had enjoyed their best season since promotion in 1985/86.

Carl Leaburn was a player reborn. He finished with 14 goals overall (11 League plus 3 cup) to finish as top scorer, just pipping Lee with 12, with all of his coming in the League.

Leaburn was at last fulfilling his potential and had added a key ingredient to his game – goals !

Charlton Career:

See Season 1996/97

1992/93   Alan Pardew

Football League – First Division*

Leading Scorer: Alan Pardew

Football League:	29+1A	9G
FA Cup:	1A	0G
League Cup:	2A	0G
Anglo-Italian Cup:	2A	1G
Total	34+1A	10G

Alan Scott Pardew

Born: Wimbledon, London, 18.7.1961

Career:
Whyteleafe
Epsom & Ewell
Corinthian Casuals
Dulwich Hamlet
Yeovil Town
Crystal Palace (FL 111+8A 8G)
Charlton Athletic (FL 98+6A 25G)
Tottenham Hotspur (loan) (FL 0A 0G)
Barnet (FL 64+3A 0G)

Honours:
Second Division Play-off winners' medal 1988/89 (with C.Palace)
FA Cup runners-up medal 1989/90 (with Crystal Palace)
Full Members Cup winners' medal 1990/91 (with Crystal Palace)

Alan Pardew, spent the early years of his career in non-league football until Crystal Palace signed him from Yeovil Town in March 1987. Palace paid a fee of £7,500 (=£21,000) for the 25 year old midfielder.

He enjoyed a successful four years at Selhurst Park, helping the Eagles win promotion to the First Division in 1989 and reach the FA Cup Final in 1990.

He moved to Charlton in November 1991 on a free transfer and, although now 30 years old, he gave the Addicks excellent service over the next four years.

Season 1992/93 saw the introduction of the FA Premier League and consequently the three remaining Football League divisions were renamed. The three divisions being rebranded as the First, Second and Third Divisions.

Charlton were therefore now in the First Division, the second tier of English football, and they started the campaign, at Upton Park, with a convincing 3-1 win against Grimsby Town. Pardew scored the winner in the next match, a 1-0 victory at Cambridge United, and repeated the feat a few days later as the Addicks edged past their landlords, West Ham United, in what was technically a 1-0 "away" win.

He then made it four goals in three matches as Bristol Rovers were eclipsed 4-1 at Upton Park with Pardew netting a brace, which included a penalty.

He was next on target in September in the Anglo-Italian Cup against Millwall at The Den. Pardew scored in the dying minutes to secure a 2-1 win for the Addicks.

Charlton had made an excellent start to the season and were unbeaten in the opening ten League matches, winning six of them. The first defeat came in October at Bristol City (1-2) and that triggered a run of three defeats. Pardew was on target in the third one, scoring twice in a bizarre 3-4 reverse at Derby County.

By this time the Addicks were closing in on their long-awaited return to The Valley. The big day finally came on 5th December when Portsmouth were beaten 1-0 to bring a successful end to an emotional occasion. Pardew was an unused substitute for this game, but he was soon back in the team as the Addicks recorded six successive draws following their homecoming.

Then came two consecutive victories in January and Pardew was on target in both. He scored twice in the 2-0 win at Bristol Rovers and then netted the winner from the penalty spot as Notts County were defeated 2-1 in SE7.

That proved to be his last goal of the season as he was injured in March and missed the last 13 matches.

Despite this, he was still top scorer with 10 goals as the Addicks finished comfortably in mid-table in 12th position.

The season will always be remembered for the triumphant return to The Valley but it should also be remembered as the first season in which a midfield player had topped Charlton's scoring charts.

The following season, 1993/94, Pardew went one better by scoring 11 times and he spent one more season at The Valley after that before departing in July 1995 to become player/coach at Barnet. Earlier that summer he had also been on loan to Tottenham Hotspur and played four matches for them in the UEFA Intertoto Cup.

In 1997 he joined Reading as Reserve Team Manager and in 1999 became their First Team Manager, which was his first step in a long managerial career.

Pardew did return to Charlton as Manager in December 2006 but was unable to save the Club from relegation from the Premier League, although results did initially improve on his arrival. He didn't manage to restore the Addicks to the top flight in the subsequent seasons and parted company with the Club in November 2008.

His managerial CV reads as follows:

Reading   1999-2003   Division 2 (Tier 3) runners-up 2002

West Ham 2003-2006 Championship Play-off winners 2005

                              FA Cup runners-up 2006

Charlton Athletic 2006-2008

Southampton 2009-2010   FL Trophy winners 2010

Newcastle Utd 2010-2014 Premier League Manager of the Season 2012

Crystal Palace 2015-2016 FA Cup runners-up 2016

West Bromwich Albion 2017-2018

ADO Den Haag 2019 - 2020

He was appointed Head Coach at Dutch side ADO Den Haag, who play in the Eridivisie (Dutch Premier Division), in December 2019 and he had as his assistant, Addicks' legend Chris Powell. However, he left the club by mutual consent in April 2020.

Charlton Career:

Seasons: 1991/92 – 1994/95

Football League: 98+6A 25G

FA Cup: 9+1A 1G

League Cup: 3+1A 0G

Anglo-Italian Cup: 6A 1G

Total: 116+8A 27G

1993/94   Carl Leaburn

Football League – First Division*

Leading Scorer: Carl Leaburn

Football League:	39A 10G
FA Cup:	6A 2G
League Cup:	2A 1G
Anglo-Italian Cup:	5+1A 3G
Total	52+1A 16G

Carl Leaburn
CHARLTON ATHLETIC FC

In a season in which Carl Leaburn would record his highest seasonal goals tally, the Addicks started brightly and were only beaten once in the opening 14 fixtures.

He scored his first League goal in August at home to Tranmere Rovers in a 3-1 victory but his next three strikes all came in cup competitions. In the Anglo-Italian Cup he was on target at Millwall where the Addicks came back from a 0-2 deficit to draw 2-2, and he then netted against Crystal Palace at The Valley in the same competition as Charlton ran out 4-1 winners.

His next goal was also against Palace, this time in the League Cup second round (1st leg) at Selhurst Park. However, the hosts took revenge for the earlier defeat and the Addicks went down 1-3, with Leaburn's goal being scant consolation.

The 14 match run in the League with only one defeat, stretched to the end of October and was followed by two defeats. A trip to Italy in the Anglo-Italian Cup was next up and Leaburn scored the equaliser against Ancona to earn a 1-1 draw.

The Addicks then recovered their form in the League by winning three successive matches, the first of these was home to Notts County who were thumped 5-1, with Leaburn hitting the first Addicks' goal.

He rounded the year off by scoring in consecutive matches. He was on target at Southend United but Charlton slumped to a 2-4 defeat. Two days later back in SE7, he netted the first goal as Stoke City were seen off 2-0.

In January, West Bromwich Albion were defeated 2-1 at The Valley with Leaburn notching the second goal, and that was followed by an FA Cup third round tie at home to Burnley who were dispatched 3-0 and he netted the second goal again.

February brought an eye-catching away win at Oxford United with the Addicks victorious by 4-0 and Leaburn scored a brace.

Charlton had enjoyed a good FA Cup run and reached the Sixth Round where they were drawn away to Manchester United at Old Trafford. Unfortunately, United were to prove too strong and the Addicks succumbed 1-3 with Leaburn scoring the consolation goal.

At the beginning of April, Southend United were the visitors to The Valley for a League match which marked the opening of the new East Stand. The match lived up to the occasion and the Addicks won a seven goal thriller 4-3 with Leaburn amongst the scorers.

Later that month he was on target in another high-scoring match in SE7. Peterborough United were dismantled 5-1 but the day really belonged to strike partner, Garry Nelson, who hit a hat-trick.

Leaburn's final goal of the campaign came at Notts County in an eventful 3-3 draw. That brought his total to 16 goals in all competitions and confirmed him as the top scorer for the second time in his Charlton career.

Garry Nelson was actually the top scorer in the League with 15 goals but Leaburn's 10 League goals were supplemented by 6 cup goals which just gave him top spot. He was also voted Player of the Year.

Charlton finished in mid-table again, this time in 11th position. Their early season results had promised much more, but patchy mid-season form, coupled with 11 defeats in their last 15 matches, brought a disappointing end to the campaign.

Charlton Career:

See Season 1996/97

1994/95   David Whyte

Football League – First Division*

Leading Scorer: David Whyte

Football League:	36+2A	19G
FA Cup:	1A	0G
League Cup:	2A	2G
Total	39+2A	21G

David Anthony Whyte

Born: Greenwich, London, 20.4.1971
Died: London, 9.9.2014

Career:
Greenwich Borough
Crystal Palace (FL 17+10A 4G)
Charlton Athletic (loan) (FL 7+1A 2G)
Charlton Athletic (FL 65+20A 28G)
Reading (FL 0A 0G)
Ipswich Town (FL 2A 0G)
Bristol Rovers (FL 0+4A 0G)
Southend United (FL 17+9A 3G)

David Whyte was a talented striker who initially joined Charlton on loan from Crystal Palace in March 1992. He made an immediate impact by scoring on his debut, hitting the winning goal in a 2-1 victory at Portsmouth. He scored again in a 2-0 win against Leicester City as the Addicks narrowly missed out on the Second Division Play-offs.

He was therefore a popular signing in July 1994 when he joined Charlton on a permanent basis from Palace. Whyte and Paul Mortimer arrived at The Valley in exchange for Darren Pitcher who moved to Selhurst Park.

Whyte was a naturally gifted striker, blessed with sublime skills and pace. He scored on his second debut for the Addicks in the first match of the 1994/95 campaign at Oldham Athletic, where the hosts inflicted a painful 2-5 defeat on the South Londoners. He was on target in the second match too, a 2-2 home draw with Barnsley.

In September he scored a brace as the Addicks edged past Bristol City 3-2 in SE7, and he then hit a real purple patch – scoring in six consecutive games.

The sequence started at Stoke City when he was on target in a 2-3 defeat and he then scored the winner back at The Valley in a 1-0 victory over Swindon Town. Swindon were also the opposition in the next match, which was in the League Cup second round (1st leg) at the County Ground, where a brace from Garry Nelson and a goal from Whyte gave the Addicks a 3-1 lead in the tie.

Back in the League and a trip to Notts County ended all square at 3-3 with Nelson (2) and Whyte again doing the honours. A few days later and it was the second leg of the League Cup tie with Swindon back in SE7. However, despite Whyte scoring, the Addicks went down 1-4, after extra time, and Swindon progressed 5-4 on aggregate.

The last match in the sequence was at home to Watford where the Addicks eased to a 3-0 victory and Whyte scored his sixth goal in six matches.

In mid-October he scored in consecutive matches again, at Port Vale in a 2-0 win, and at home to Burnley in a 1-2 reverse. Injury caused him to miss most of the matches in November but he was back in the starting line-up in December and scored in consecutive home victories against Oldham Athletic (2-0) and Southend United (3-1).

At the turn of the year, Whyte's goal total stood at 14.

He continued his good form into January and was again on target in three consecutive matches. He scored the only goal as the Addicks won 1-0 at Luton Town and then scored at The Valley against Derby County, where the hosts' 3-1 interval lead dissolved into a 3-4 defeat. As if that wasn't painful enough, the following week Whyte's goal was all Charlton had to show from their visit to Bolton Wanderers where they slumped to a 1-5 defeat.

The Addicks bounced back from that setback with two victories in February, in the second of which Whyte netted the only goal at home to Sunderland to secure all three points in a 1-0 win.

He then hit a barren patch and did not score for 11 games, although he was out injured for four of them, but he returned to form in April, scoring in three consecutive matches.

First up were Wolverhampton Wanderers in SE7 and Whyte opened the scoring in a 3-2 victory. He then put the Addicks ahead at Southend United but the hosts bounced back to inflict a 1-2 defeat. His final goal of the season came, fittingly, at home and it was another winning strike as the Addicks edged past Luton Town 1-0.

That brought Whyte's total to 21 goals making him top scorer by some distance, Nelson being closest to him with 9. Whyte's total was also the most goals by a Charlton player since Derek Hales netted 23 in 1980/81.

However, Charlton experienced another mediocre season, finishing in a disappointing 15th place.

Charlton Career:

See Season 1996/97

1995/96 Lee Bowyer

Football League – First Division*

Leading Scorer: Lee Bowyer

Football League:	41A	8G
FA Cup:	3A	1G
League Cup:	6A	5G
Play-offs:	2A	0G
Total	52A	14G

Lee David Bowyer

Born: Canning Town, London, 3.1.1977

Career:
Senrab
Charlton Athletic (FL 46A 8G)
Leeds United (PL 196+7A 38G)
West Ham United (PL 10A 0G)
Newcastle United (PL 61+18A 6G)
West Ham United (PL 34+7A 4G)
Birmingham City (FL/PL 75+6A 10G)
Ipswich Town (FL 24+5A 2G)

Honours
England Youth – 6 caps (with Charlton)
England U21 – 8 caps – 4G (4 caps with Charlton, 4 with Leeds Utd)
England Full International – 1 cap v Portugal 2002 (with Leeds Utd)
FL Championship* runners-up 2008/09 (with Birmingham City)
Football League Cup winners' medal 2011 (with Birmingham City)
(*Tier 2)

Lee Bowyer was another product of Charlton's youth system and was signed as a professional in April 1994. A skillful, competitive, goal-scoring midfielder, he made his debut during the 1994/95 campaign but became a fixture in the team in 1995/96 at the tender age of 18.

Although the Addicks lost their opening match (0-1 at West Bromwich Albion), they were undefeated in the next six and Bowyer was on target in four successive games.

It started with the home League victory over Birmingham City (3-1) and he then scored twice against Barnet in the League Cup first round (2nd leg) at

The Valley to send Charlton through 2-0 on aggregate. He hit the net again at Crystal Palace (1-1) and at home to Watford (2-1). So in the first five matches of the season he had already notched five goals.

In September the Addicks were drawn against Wimbledon in the League Cup second round, with the 1st Leg being played away at Selhurst Park, as Wimbledon were now ground-sharing with Crystal Palace. In a high-scoring encounter, Charlton eventually triumphed 5-4 and Bowyer hit a memorable hat-trick. The 2nd leg in SE7 was another goal-fest which finished 3-3 (aet) so the Addicks advanced 8-7 on aggregate.

By the turn of the year, Bowyer had brought his total up to 10 goals with strikes in the home games against Norwich City (1-1) in October and Port Vale (2-2) in November.

In December the Addicks recorded a memorable 2-0 victory at Millwall on a snowy evening. Unfortunately, Bowyer was sent-off after 20 minutes for two bookable offences, although the numbers were evened up in the second-half with the Lions also being reduced to ten men thanks to a straight red card.

Bowyer's next goal came in February in the FA Cup fourth round as Charlton edged past Brentford 3-2 at The Valley. He then hit the winning goal in the next match, at Watford, to secure a 2-1 victory.

Later that month he was on target at Huddersfield Town where the Addicks recovered from 0-2 to take a point in a 2-2 draw. His final goal of the campaign came at The Valley in March and it was a significant strike. He scored in the fifth minute of the local derby with Millwall to set up a 2-0 win and record a rare double over the Lions.

Charlton had enjoyed a good season, finishing in sixth place and qualifying for the Play-offs. Crystal Palace were their opponents in the semi-final but two narrow defeats (1-2 and 0-1) resulted in the Eagles advancing to the final.

Bowyer, in his first full season in the First Team, finished as top-scorer with 14 goals, emulating fellow midfielder Alan Pardew in 1992/93 but eclipsing his 10 goals. He also won four England U21 caps and, such was his form, that Premier Division clubs were inevitably taking an interest in the precocious talent.

As had happened so many times in the past, and since, no sooner had the Valley faithfully found themselves a new young hero, he was snatched away from them. Leeds United paid a then record fee for a teenager of £2,812,500 (=£5.3m) to take Bowyer to Elland Road in July 1996.

He went on to enjoy a glittering career with Leeds playing in the Premier League, UEFA Champions League and the UEFA Cup. He was also voted their Player of the Year on two occasions and won a Full England cap.

After more than six years at Elland Road, he continued his Premier League career at West Ham United, who he joined in January 2003, and then at Newcastle United, signing for them in July of the same year. He spent three years at St James' Park before rejoining West Ham in June 2006.

In January 2009 he moved to Birmingham City and helped them achieve promotion to the Premier League at the end of that season by clinching the runners-up spot in the Football League Championship. He enjoyed two seasons at St Andrew's which culminated in winning the League Cup at Wembley in 2011.

In July 2011 he made his last move, to Ipswich Town, spending one season at Portman Road before retiring in 2012, aged 35.

Bowyer began his coaching career at Watford in 2015, with their U21's but he then returned to The Valley as a coach and became Assistant Manager under Karl Robinson in 2017. When Robinson resigned in March 2018, Bowyer was appointed Caretaker Manager and led the Addicks to the League One Play-offs, although Charlton lost out to Shrewsbury Town in the semi-final.

Bowyer was eventually appointed officially as Manager in September 2018 and took the Addicks to a third place finish in League One in 2018/19, and another tilt at the Play-offs. This time they made it to Wembley where they defeated Sunderland 2-1, with a last minute winner, to reclaim their place in the Championship.

Lee Bowyer's career has gone full circle. He is back at Charlton, where it all started for him, and is now carving out a management career which we hope will be as successful as his playing career.

Charlton Career:

Seasons: 1994/95 – 1995/96

Football League: 46A 8G

FA Cup: 3A 1G

League Cup: 6+1A 5G

Play-Offs: 2A 0G

Total: 57+1A 14G

1996/97 Carl Leaburn & David Whyte

Football League – First Division*

Leading Scorers: Carl Leaburn & David Whyte

Carl Leaburn

Football League:		40+4A	8G
FA Cup:		2A	0G
League Cup:		4A	1G
	Total	46+4A	9G

Carl Leaburn
CHARLTON ATHLETIC FC

Charlton made a slow start to the 1996/97 campaign, only gaining one point from the opening four fixtures when Carl Leaburn scored the equaliser in a 1-1 Valley draw with West Bromwich Albion.

He was then on target in consecutive home matches in September, hitting the winner in the 1-0 victory over Reading and then scoring in the League Cup second round (1st leg) against Burnley who suffered a 4-1 mauling.

His next strike was also in SE7, in October, as the Addicks eased past Oxford United 2-0 and he added just one more goal before the turn of the year, netting against Swindon Town in December in another 2-0 home victory.

In the second half of the season he scored four times, all of them at The Valley. February saw him on the scoresheet against Tranmere Rovers in a 3-1 triumph and he was also amongst the scorers in a bizarre 4-4 draw with Norwich City.

In March, Charlton had to come from behind at home against Queens Park Rangers, with Leaburn netting the equaliser which paved the way to a 2-1 victory.

His final goal of the season came in April, against Manchester City in a 1-1 draw, which brought his total to 9 goals. This was the third time he had finished as top marksman, but this time he had to share the honours with David Whyte.

Charlton finished in a disappointing 15th place, a big drop from the 6th place finish the previous year.

Leaburn's Valley career continued into the next season, 1997/98, but he was struggling to hold down a regular place in the team mainly due to the arrival of strikers Clive Mendonca and Steve Jones.

He did, however, hit three goals in 13 League starts to contribute towards the Addicks', ultimately successful, bid for promotion.

After more than 10 years with Charlton, Leaburn moved to Premier League club Wimbledon for a £300,000 (=£530,000) fee in January 1998. He stayed with the Dons until December 2001, when he signed for Queens Park Rangers.

His stay at Loftus Road was brief and he moved into non-league football with Grays Athletic in December 2002, before retiring in 2005 aged 36.

After a slow start to his career, Carl Leaburn became a cult figure at The Valley for 10 years. Popular with players and fans alike, his playing record of 376 matches and 66 goals puts him in 13th place in both the all-time appearances and goal-scoring charts.

Charlton Career:

Seasons: 1986/87 – 1997/98

Football League: 276+46A 53G

FA Cup: 19+2A 4G

League Cup: 19A 5G

Full Members Cup: 1+2A 0G

Anglo-Italian Cup: 6+2A 4G

Play-Offs: 2+1A 0G

Total: 323+53A 66G

David Whyte

Football League: 18+4A 7G

FA Cup: 2A 0G

League Cup: 1+2A 2G

                    Total   21+6A 9G

David Whyte
CHARLTON ATHLETIC FC

Following his stellar performance in 1994/95, when he netted 21 goals, David Whyte had a lot to live up to in subsequent seasons.

Unfortunately injuries limited his appearances, and therefore goals, but he did manage to share top spot in 1996/97, which proved to be his last season at The Valley.

His first goal came in September in the League Cup second round (2nd leg) at Burnley. The Addicks were already 4-1 up from the 1st leg but Whyte came on as substitute after 88 minutes and scored two minutes later to secure a 2-1 victory at Turf Moor and send Charlton through, convincingly, 6-2 on aggregate.

He was a 'super-sub' in the next match too against Oldham Athletic at The Valley, coming on late in the game and scoring four minutes from time to secure a 1-0 victory.

In October he scored a brace at home to Bolton Wanderers in a 3-3 draw, a match in which the hosts squandered a 3-1 lead. Probably his best goal came in the League Cup third round at home to Liverpool when he put the Addicks ahead with a spectacular long range strike. Unfortunately, Liverpool equalised three minute later and the match finished 1-1. It was a lost opportunity as Charlton went down 1-4 at Anfield in the replay.

He missed most of November through injury but returned at the end of the month against Grimsby Town in SE7 and duly scored. Unfortunately, the Mariners netted three times, including a brace from a certain Clive Mendonca, to inflict a 1-3 defeat on the South Londoners. Whyte was on target in the next match at Oxford United where the Addicks triumphed 2-0.

In December he brought his total up to eight goals when he scored, along with Leaburn, as the Addicks eased past Swindon Town 2-0 at The Valley.

In January he netted a late equaliser at Reading to earn a 2-2 draw and that was his ninth goal. It proved to be his last of the season……….and his last for the Club.

Due to injury, he did not play beyond January and missed the last 18 League matches on the season. However, his total of 9 goals from only 21 starts was still a reasonable return.

In September 1997 he was released and after spending a month on trial at Reading, he signed for Ipswich Town. He only made a few appearances for them before moving to Bristol Rovers in January 1998. It was another brief stay and he moved again March 1998 and joined Southend United.

He spent a year at Roots Hall before retiring in February 1999, aged only 28.

David Whyte was a naturally gifted player, as Addicks' fans who witnessed his 21 goal haul in 1994/95 will testify. However, he never really managed to fulfill his potential and drifted out of the game far too early.

A tragic footnote is that David passed away, aged only 43, in September 2014.

Charlton career:

Seasons: 1991/92, 1994/95 – 1996/97

Football League: 72+21A 30G

FA Cup: 3+1A 1G

League Cup: 5+2A 4G

Play-Offs: 0+2A 0G

Total: 80+26A 35G

1997/98   Clive Mendonca

Football League – First Division*

Leading Scorer: Clive Mendonca

Football League:	40A	23G
FA Cup:	2A	1G
League Cup:	2A	1G
Play-offs:	<u>2A</u>	<u>3G</u>
Total	46A	28G

Clive Paul Mendonca

Born: Islington, London, 9.9.1968

Career:
Sheffield United (FL 8+5A 4G)
Doncaster Rovers (loan) (FL 2A 0G)
Rotherham United (FL 71+13A 27G)
Sheffield United (FL 4+6A 1G)
Grimsby Town (loan) (FL 10A 3G)
Grimsby Town (FL 151+5A 58G)
Charlton Athletic (FL/PL 78+6A 40G)

Honours
First Division*Play-off winners' medal 1997/98 (with Charlton)
First Division*Champions medal 1999/2000 (with Charlton)
(*Tier 2)

Clive Mendonca was born in London and brought up in Sunderland but he started his football career with Sheffield United in September 1986.

Being unable to command a regular place with the Blades, he spent a month on loan spell at Doncaster Rovers in February 1988 and then made a permanent move to Rotherham United in March 1988 for a fee of £35,000 (=£95,000). It was with the Millers that he gained a reputation as a predatory goal-scorer, so much so that Sheffield United brought him back to Bramall Lane in August 1991, paying a fee of £110,000 (=£240,000).

However, he still found himself on the fringes of the Blades' team and in January 1992 he went on loan to Grimsby Town where he impressed enough to earn a permanent move in June 1992, with the Mariners parting with £85,000 (=£180,000). He was immensely popular on Humberside and enjoyed a great five years at Blundell Park, scoring 66 League and cup goals. One of the clubs he usually managed to score against was Charlton, so he was a popular signing when he joined the Addicks in May 1997 for a Club record fee of £700,000 (=£1.2m). It proved to be an inspired piece of business.

Mendonca opened his account in the second match of the season, a 3-2 home victory over Oxford United, and was also on target in the League Cup second round (2nd leg) at Ipswich Town where the Addicks went down 1-3.

In September he hit five goals in two matches, starting with a hat-trick at Norwich City in a 4-0 mauling of the Canaries, and he then netted a brace at The Valley as Bradford City were dispatched 4-1.

The goals continued to flow in October with him scoring in an impressive 3-0 win at Huddersfield Town and at home to Birmingham City, which finished 1-1.

November opened with another Mendonca strike as Ipswich Town were beaten 3-0 in SE7, but then an injury sidelined him for three matches that month. He returned against Swindon Town at The Valley and scored twice, one being a penalty, in a 3-0 win. He replicated that in December against Sheffield United, scoring twice, with one being a spot kick, in a 2-1 home victory.

At the turn of the year he had 14 goals to his name and his next strike came in the FA Cup third round. Nottingham Forest were the visitors to the Valley and were blitzed 4-1, with Mendonca netting the fourth goal.

In January, Charlton had to come from behind to win 2-1 at Oxford United and it was Mendonca who notched the late equaliser to set up the away victory. He then missed a few more matches through injury but was back in the side by the time March dawned and he was on target in consecutive matches.

West Bromwich Albion were dismantled 5-0 in SE7 with Mendonca netting twice, once from the spot, and he then put the Addicks ahead at Ipswich Town but the hosts hit back to inflict a 1-3 defeat.

The Addicks then went on a 10 match unbeaten run, which included eight consecutive victories, up to the end of the season. Mendonca was on target in five of those wins starting with a penalty as Nottingham Forest were edged out 4-2 at The Valley.

He then scored in the home wins against Wolverhampton Wanderers (1-0) and Reading (3-0) before netting a vital penalty at Port Vale to secure a 1-0 victory. He then converted two penalties in the last home game to ease past Tranmere Rovers 2-0.

That brought his total to 25 goals but, as the Addicks had secured fourth place, they still had the Play-offs to come and a chance to reach the Premier League.

Ipswich Town were defeated 1-0 home and away in the semi-final so the Addicks went through 2-0 on aggregate.

The Wembley final was against Sunderland and provided Mendonca with his finest hour. In one of the greatest games ever seen at the historic stadium, the teams fought out a thrilling 3-3 draw after 90 minutes, and it was 4-4 after extra time. Mendonca scored a memorable hat-trick and, when the match went to penalties, he netted one of those too as the Addicks won the shoot-out 7-6 and promotion to the Premier League.

Mendonca's total of 28 goals was the highest by a Charlton player for 22 years, when Derek Hales hit 31 in 1975/76.

Charlton Career:

See Season 1998/99

1998/99   Clive Mendonca

FA Premier League

Leading Scorer: Clive Mendonca

Premier League:	19+6A	8G
FA Cup:	0A	0G
League Cup:	<u>3A</u>	<u>0G</u>
Total	22+6A	8G

Charlton's first season in the Premier League started well with a win and two draws in their opening three matches. It started well for Clive Mendonca too as he scored a hat-trick, including a penalty, in the second match when Southampton thumped 5-0 at The Valley.

In September he was on target in successive games, at home to Derby County when he netted another penalty in a 1-2 defeat, and at Liverpool in a thrilling 3-3 draw.

In mid-November he scored another penalty at home to Middlesbrough in a 1-1 draw and up to that point the Addicks had been coping well in the top tier. However, following that draw, they hit a poor run of form and lost eight matches in a row.

Worse still, Mendonca was injured in December and missed seven matches, only returning, as a substitute, in the 2-0 victory at Derby County in February. He was eased back in from the bench over the next few games, and came on to score a last minute equaliser at Leicester City in March to snatch a 1-1 draw.

Charlton were struggling without their main goal-scorer and he missed another five games following his Leicester heroics. He returned to the starting line-up in the penultimate match at Aston Villa. Charlton had to win to have any chance of avoiding the drop and they duly did just that in dramatic style, winning 4-3 with Mendonca among the scorers.

The last match at home to Sheffield Wednesday was also a must win game but the Addicks went down 0-1 and lost their battle against relegation.

They finished 18th and, as disappointing a relegation was, they had at least fought to the last match before their fate was finally sealed.

The loss of Mendonca for half the season, he only started 19 League matches, was a major factor in their demise. His return of 8 goals in those matches still represented a good strike rate.

In the following season (1999/2000), back in the First Division, Mendonca was still troubled by his hip injury and again only played in 19 League matches. As the Addicks returned to the Premier League at the first attempt, he still hit 9 goals to finish as second highest scorer behind Andy Hunt.

Sadly he did not play again as he was unable to overcome his injury and he finally announced his retirement in February 2002. He returned to live in Sunderland where he now works for Nissan.

Charlton played a testimonial match for him in August 2003 against Dutch side NEC Nijmegen and in 2012 he was inducted into the **Charlton Hall of Fame.**

Clive Mendonca only played for Charlton for three seasons but he made a seismic impact in a short space of time and his Wembley hat-trick will never be forgotten.

Charlton Career:

Seasons: 1997/98 – 1999/2000

Football League/Premier League: 78+6A 40G

FA Cup: 3A 1G

League Cup: 6+1A 1G

Play-Offs: 2A 3G

Total: 89+7A 45G

1999/00   Andy Hunt

Football League – First Division*

Leading Scorer: Andy Hunt

Football League: 43+1A 24G

FA Cup: 4A 1G

League Cup: <u>1A 0G</u>

Total 48+1A 25G

Andy Hunt
CHARLTON ATHLETIC FC

Andrew Hunt

Born: West Thurrock, Essex, 9.6.1970

Career:
Kings Lynn
Kettering Town
Newcastle United (FL 34+9A 11G)
West Bromwich Albion (FL 201+11A 76G)
Charlton Athletic (FL/PL 83+3A 35G)

Honours:
Second Division (Tier 3) Play-off winners' medal 1993 (with WBA)
First Division* Champions medal 1999/2000 (with Charlton)
(*Tier 2)

Essex born Andy Hunt started his career in non-league football with Kings Lynn and Kettering Town. Newcastle United spotted his potential and paid Kettering £169,000 (=£365,000) for the young striker in January 1991.

He spent two years at St James' Park and then moved to West Bromwich Albion for a fee of £113,000 (=£230,000) in March 1993. He made an immediate impact at The Hawthorns, scoring at Wembley in the 1992/93 Second Division (Tier 3) Play-off final as Albion beat Port Vale 3-0.

He had five successful seasons with Albion, forming a prolific partnership with Bob Taylor, before joining Charlton in July 1998. No fee was involved as he had allowed his contract to run out. The Addicks had just been promoted to the Premier League so he at last had the chance to play at the highest level.

Of course, that first season in the Premier League didn't go to plan and the Addicks were relegated at the end of the 1998/99 campaign, Hunt scoring seven times in his first season at the top level. However, it was Hunt who made it possible for the Club to make a quick return as he enjoyed the best season of his career in 1999/2000 in the First Division*.

The early headlines were made by his strike partner, Clive Mendonca, who netted a hat-trick in the opening game, a 3-1 victory over Barnsley. But Hunt was not to be denied, and in the fifth match he opened his account by scoring both goals to defeat Sheffield United 2-1 at Bramall Lane.

Two weeks later he eclipsed that by hitting a hat-trick as Stockport County were demolished 4-0 at The Valley. Going into October, he scored another brace at Ipswich Town, although it was not enough to secure the points as the Addicks went down 2-4.

Goals in successive games in November, at home to Walsall (2-1) and in an eye-catching 5-2 victory at Grimsby Town, brought his total to nine. In the second half of the season he was to more than double that.

Charlton were in fine form and when they defeated Crystal Palace 2-1 in SE7 on Boxing Day, it was the start of a record-breaking run of 12 consecutive League victories. Hunt was at his most prolific during this spell, scoring 11 times and even adding a 12th in the FA Cup.

His run started with a goal at Huddersfield Town at the end of December in a 2-1 triumph for the Addicks, and he was also on target in the first match of the New Year as Nottingham Forest were dispatched 3-0 at The Valley.

He then scored in three consecutive matches starting with the FA Cup fifth round tie at Coventry City where the Addicks came back from 0-2 down to win 3-2, with Hunt hitting the late winner. Back in the League, he netted a hat-trick at Norwich City in a 3-0 victory and repeated the dose in the next match, at Stockport County, where the Addicks won 3-1 and Hunt netted his third hat-trick of the season, and his second against Stockport. He had now scored seven goals in three consecutive away matches.

March was another productive month for Hunt as he scored at Bolton Wanderers (2-0) and twice at Walsall (4-2) in the record-breaking twelfth consecutive victory. He also scored at The Valley as Grimsby Town were overcome 4-0.

With Charlton sitting on top of the First Division* table going into April, they only needed a few points to be crowned champions, but, as so often happens, they just could not get the wins they needed to clinch the title.

Hunt scored at Port Vale but they had to settle for a 2-2 draw, and it was a similar story four days later at Nottingham Forest where his strike was canceled out by a late equaliser resulting in another draw (1-1).

One point from the next two matches still had the Addicks' nerves twitching but the breakthrough came in the next match at Blackburn Rovers. Although that too ended in a 1-1 draw, results elsewhere confirmed Charlton as champions. It was their first championship since 1935, their other promotions coming from second or third place.

The final home match of the season a week later was against fellow promotion candidates Ipswich Town. In a carnival atmosphere at The Valley Hunt scored his 25th goal of the season. However, Ipswich hadn't read the script and took the points by inflicting a 1-3 defeat on the new champions. The trophy and medals were presented after the game and even the defeat could not dampen the party mood.

Andy Hunt's total of 25 goals included 24 in the League, thereby eclipsing Clive Mendonca's 23 goal haul in the League in 1997/98.

Hunt now had another chance to test himself in the Premier League.

Charlton made a good start to the 2000/01 campaign, only losing twice in the opening eight fixtures. Hunt had scored four times including a brace at Highbury in an eight goal thriller which the Addicks eventually lost 3-5.

But all was not well with Hunt. He was struggling with a "flu-like bug" and was exhausted in training and was having trouble completing matches. In the eighth game of the season, at home to Coventry City, it came to a head. Charlton were trailing 0-1 when the ball arrived at Hunt's feet in the penalty area and he duly netted the equaliser. But he was once again totally exhausted and was immediately substituted. It proved to be his last goal and last appearance for the Club.

His problem was eventually diagnosed as Chronic Fatigue Syndrome and he had to announce his retirement in July 2001.

This was a terrible blow both to him and to Charlton. He was in his prime and to have to retire in this way was such a cruel ending to his career. Charlton had now lost two quality strikers, both having to retire prematurely, Mendonca through injury and Hunt through illness, in the space of a year.

Andy now lives in Belize in Central America where he and his wife run two adventure travel companies.

Charlton Career:

Seasons: 1998/99 – 2000/01

Football League/Premier League: 83+3A 35G

FA Cup: 5A 1G

League Cup: 3A 0G

Total: 91+3A 36G

2000/01 Jonatan Johansson

FA Premier League

Leading Scorer: Jonatan Johansson

Premier League:	27+4A	11G
FA Cup:	0A	0G
League Cup:	2A	3G
Total	29+4A	14G

Jonatan Johansson
CHARLTON ATHLETIC FC

Jonatan Lillebror Johansson

Born: Stockholm, Sweden, 16.8.1975

Career:
Pargas IF (Finland)
TPS (Finland)
FC Flora (Estonia)
Glasgow Rangers (SL 22+25A 14G)
Charlton Athletic (PL 90+58A 27G)
Norwich City (loan) (FL 6+6A 3G)
Malmo FF (Sweden)
Hibernian (SL 5+4A 0G)
St Johnstone (SL 2+4A 1G)
TPS (Finland)

Honours:
Finish Cup runners-up medal 1996 (with TPS)
Finish Cup winners' medal 2010 (with TPS)
Estonian League runners-up 1997 (with FC Flora)
Scottish Premier League winners' medal 1998/99 (with Rangers)
Scottish FA Cup winners' medal 1998/99 (with Rangers)
Scottish League Cup winners' medal 1998/99 (with Rangers)
Scottish Premier League winners' medal 1999/00 (with Rangers)
Scottish FA Cup winners' medal 1999/00 (with Rangers)
Finland U21 – 7 caps
Finland Full International – 105 caps-22G (42 caps with Charlton)

Although being born in Sweden, Jonatan Johansson was a Finnish national and started his career in Finland with Pargas IF in 1994. In 1995 he moved to another Finnish club, TPS Turku, where his performances brought him his first international recognition in the form of caps for Finland U21.

In August 1996 he transferred to Estonian club FC Flora, in Tallinn, where he caught the attention of Glasgow Rangers. In August 1997, Rangers paid £500,000 (=£900,000) to bring the young striker into the Scottish Premier League.

He enjoyed a successful three years with Rangers, winning both the treble and the double with the Ibrox club, before Charlton paid a fee of £3.75m (=£6.3m) in August 2000 to bring him to The Valley.

The Addicks had just returned to the Premier League for 2000/01 and Johansson was seen as key signing to help to keep them there.

He was by this time an established Full international with Finland and had European competition experience with Rangers. His main assets were his pace and finishing (no pun intended) ability, and he turned out to be a shrewd and popular signing for the Addicks.

He didn't figure in the opening two matches of the season through injury but made his debut, from the bench, in the third match at Arsenal in a 3-5 defeat. The next match was at home to Southampton, where he again came off the bench, and snatched a late equaliser in a 1-1 draw.

That was the start of a seven match run in which he netted seven goals. His next strike came at Derby County (2-2) and he then hit the only goal of the game as Tottenham Hotspur were defeated 1-0 at The Valley.

Next up was the League Cup second round (1st leg) at Stoke City where he scored in a 1-2 defeat. Back in the League, the Addicks won 1-0 at Newcastle United, with Graham Stuart netting the winner, but Johansson was back on target a few days later when Stoke visited SE7 for the second leg of the League Cup tie.

He scored a brace as the Addicks won 4-3, after extra time, but although the aggregate score was level at 5-5, the Potters went through on away goals. His seventh goal in this sequence came at home to Coventry City where his late equaliser secured a point in a 2-2 draw.

The Charlton fans now knew that they had a new hero and he was bestowed with an appropriate nickname, "JJ".

In November he was on target in two home wins, against Bradford City (2-0) and Chelsea, also 2-0, and in December he gave the Addicks the lead at Leicester City but the hosts eventually prevailed to inflict a 1-3 defeat. He then netted twice in the last match of the year at Manchester City where the Addicks triumphed 4-1.

His total now stood at 12 goals and he added to that on New Year's Day by hitting the winner at The Valley in a 1-0 victory over Arsenal. He was then sidelined for the next four matches but returned to the team in February and scored at Coventry City in a 2-2 draw.

That proved to be his last goal of the campaign but his 14 goals meant that he was the only Charlton player to hit double figures and was comfortably top scorer.

Charlton finished in ninth position, which was more than satisfactory for their first season back in the top flight.

"JJ" remained at The Valley for another five seasons, all in the Premier League, and had a loan spell with Norwich City in January 2006 prior to his departure to Swedish club Malmo, in July 2006, who paid a fee of £990,000 (=£1.4m).

In January 2009, he returned to Scotland and signed for Hibernian before moving to St Johnstone in October 2009. He returned to his old club, TPS in Finland, in January 2010 before finally retiring in March 2011, aged 35.

He then embarked on a coaching and management career which started at Greenock Morton (U20's) in 2012 and he then moved to coach Motherwell's

U20's until 2015. In 2016 he was appointed as Assistant Manager to the Finland national team before leaving that position in April 2017 to return to Glasgow Rangers as Assistant Manager. In September 2018, he was appointed as Manager of Greenock Morton but left the club at the end of the 2018/19 season.

"JJ" enjoyed a magnificent career which spanned five different countries and he also has the second highest number of international appearances for Finland, winning 105 caps. The 42 caps gained while with Charlton makes him the Addicks' joint most capped player (along with Radostin Kishishev of Bulgaria).

Charlton Career:

Seasons: 2000/01 – 2005/06

Premier League: 90+58A 27G

FA Cup: 5+3A 2G

League Cup: 9+2A 4G

Total: 104+63A 33G

2001/02   Jason Euell

FA Premier League

Leading Scorer: Jason Euell

Premier League:	31+5A	11G
FA Cup:	2A	1G
League Cup:	2A	1G
Total	35+5A	13G

Jason Euell
CHARLTON ATHLETIC FC

Jason Joseph Euell

Born: Lambeth, London, 6.2.1977

Career:
Wimbledon (PL/FL 118+23A 41G)
Charlton Athletic (PL 102+37A 34G)
Middlesbrough (PL 9+8A 0G)
Southampton (FL 49+13A 5G)
Blackpool (FL/PL 24+12A 4G)
Doncaster Rovers (loan) (FL 7+5A 3G)
Charlton Athletic (FL 0+11A 0G)
AFC Wimbledon (loan) (FL 8+1A 0G)

Honours:
England U20 – 2 caps (with Wimbledon)
England U21 – 6 caps (with Wimbledon)
Jamaica Full International – 3 caps – 1 goal (with Charlton)
FL Championship Play-off winners' medal 2009/10 (with Blackpool)
FL League One Champions medal 2011/12 (with Charlton)

Jason Euell's career started at Wimbledon, developing in their youth system to sign professional in June 1995. He spent six years with the Dons, five of them in the Premier League, before signing for Charlton in July 2001 for a then Club record fee of £4.75m (=£7.9m).

The Addicks were just embarking on their second season back in the Premier League in 2001/02 and he was competing for a starting place along with the likes of Jonatan Johansson, Shaun Bartlett and Kevin Lisbie.

He figured in the opening six League matches but did not score his first goal until October in the League Cup. Drawn away to West Bromwich Albion in the third round, the Addicks won 1-0 with Euell getting off the mark via the penalty spot. Two matches later, he came off the bench at Derby County to net a late equaliser in a 1-1 draw to record his first League goal for the Club.

In November he was on target in successive matches, both high scoring encounters. First Charlton chalked up a memorable 4-2 win at Arsenal, their first victory at Highbury since 1956, and it was Euell who notched the fourth goal. He then scored twice in the next match at home to West Ham United which eventually finished with a bizarre 4-4 score-line.

He then missed a couple of games due to a family bereavement but was back in the team in December and hit a rich vein on form over the New Year period. The last match of the year was at Everton and the Addicks came away with an impressive 3-0 victory with Euell supplying one of the goals.

On New Year's Day he was on target again as Charlton came back from 0-2 down to Ipswich Town at The Valley, to win 3-2, with Euell netting the winner. A few days later in the FA Cup third round against Blackpool in SE7, he repeated the feat as the Addicks again came from behind to win 2-1, with Euell providing the decisive strike. His fourth goal in four matches came at Blackburn Rovers but it was only a consolation in a dismal 1-4 defeat.

March was another fertile period for him and he scored in the opening two matches. He hit a brace as the Addicks edged past Chelsea 2-1 at The Valley and then scored the equaliser at Leicester City in a 1-1 draw.

After looking certain of a top-half finish, the Addicks tailed away and failed to register a win in the final eight matches. Euell did manage to add one more goal to his total in the penultimate match at home to Sunderland, scoring after just 64 seconds in the 2-2 draw.

That brought his total to 13 goals in his first season at The Valley and, although the Addicks eventually finished in a disappointing 14th position, there was still a lot more to come from Jason Euell.

Charlton Career:

See Season 2003/04

2002/03 Jason Euell

FA Premier League

Leading Scorer: Jason Euell

Premier League: 35+1A 10G

FA Cup   2A   1G

League Cup: 1A   0G

Total 38+1A 11G

The Addicks' third season in the top tier did not start well. In the opening match at home to Chelsea they squandered a 2-0 lead and lost 2-3. They did recover from that a week later at Bolton Wanderers where they came back from a goal down to win 2-1, with Jason Euell netting the winner.

However, the poor form continued and only three wins were recorded in the opening 13 League games. One of those victories came in October when a strike from Euell brought a much needed 1-0 win against Middlesbrough at The Valley.

From November, Euell was switched to a deeper midfield role and the change seemed to benefit both him and the team. Having only won three matches up to mid-November, the Addicks then went on a 15 match run in which they only lost once and recorded 10 victories.

Despite his midfield role, Euell was still a regular on the scoresheet and his next goal came against Blackburn Rovers who were defeated 3-1 in SE7. He then scored in successive home matches in December, first against Liverpool who were beaten 2-0, and he then netted a penalty as Manchester City went home with a point from a 2-2 draw.

On Boxing Day, Euell scored twice at Tottenham Hotspur to give the Addicks a 2-0 lead, so it was disappointing, to say the least, when two late Spurs' goals levelled things up at 2-2.

He was next on target in early January in the home FA Cup third round tie with Exeter City. The visitors put in a good performance and it wasn't until Euell's late penalty, to make the score 3-1, that the Addicks' fans could finally relax.

He hit his ninth goal of the season in the next match at Chelsea. It was also a penalty but was scant consolation as the Addicks went down 1-4, bringing their nine match unbeaten run to an end. The defeat didn't seem to affect them, however, as they were unbeaten in the next six matches, five of which were won. Euell was on target in the last match of that sequence, at the end of February, as the Addicks eased past Aston Villa 3-0 at The Valley.

From March onwards, the good form suddenly evaporated and only one win was obtained from the last 10 matches. Euell was on target in one of those games when he netted a penalty against Leeds United in SE7, but the Addicks were completely out-classed and went down to an eye-watering 1-6 defeat.

That was his 11th goal of the season and he was again top scorer despite playing in a midfield role for more than half the season. Indeed he was the only player to reach double figures for the second season running.

Charlton again finished mid-table, in 12th position, which, given their poor start to the season, was something of a relief.

Charlton Career:

See Season 2003/04

2003/04 Jason Euell

FA Premier League
Leading Scorer: Jason Euell

Premier League:	24+7A	10G
FA Cup:	0+1A	0G
League Cup:	<u>1+1A</u>	<u>0G</u>
Total	25+9A	10G

Jason Euell started the 2003/04 campaign in midfield in the opening day defeat to Manchester City at The Valley (0-3).

He was restored to his striker position for the next match at Wolverhampton Wanderers where he scored the Addicks' first goal of the season as they romped to an emphatic 4-0 victory. He was on target in the next match too as he converted two penalties against Everton in a 2-2 home draw.

For the next few months he remained up front, often being paired with new signing Paulo Di Canio, before being switched to midfield again for the Boxing Day clash with Chelsea at The Valley. Charlton produced one of their finest performances to win 4-2 and Euell duly notched the fourth goal.

He remained in his midfield role for the rest of the season and scored a brace against Wolverhampton Wanderers in January to secure a 2-0 home victory. In February he provided one of the goals as Blackburn Rovers were edged out 3-2 in SE7.

Going into the last two matches of the season, he was still stuck on seven goals. Then, in the penultimate game at Leeds United, the Addicks were 1-3 down with time running out when they were awarded a penalty. Euell stepped up and dispatched it to reduce the arears, and three minutes later he hit the equaliser to earn a 3-3 draw.

The last match was at The Valley against Southampton and Euell opened the scoring to set up a 2-1 victory.

That brought his total to 10 goals and he was top scorer for the third season running and again the only player to achieve double figures. Charlton finished in 7th position to achieve their highest finish in the Premier League.

Euell stayed with Charlton for another two seasons but was not able to replicate the scoring record from his first three seasons. Being unable to command a regular place in the team, he moved to Middlesbrough in August 2006 for a fee of £300,000 (=£440,000) where he continued his Premier League career.

In August 2007 he returned south to join Southampton, who were in the Championship, and after two seasons with the Saints he was transferred to another Championship club, Blackpool, in September 2009. He helped them to gain promotion to the Premier League by winning the Championship Play-offs in 2010.

He had a loan spell with Doncaster Rovers in February 2011 but then returned to Charlton in August 2011 and became part of Chris Powell's squad that won the League One Title with a record number of points (101). All his League appearances that season were from the bench but his quality and experience were invaluable in helping to clinch the championship.

During that season he returned to his roots, by joining AFC Wimbledon (the successor to his first club) on loan in January 2012.

Jason retired at the end of the 20011/12 season and then commenced his coaching career. He became a Charlton Academy coach in 2013 and is currently the Club's U23 coach. He is highly qualified having now attained the FA Level 5 (UEFA Pro) Licence.

He has been instrumental in bringing a succession of academy graduates through to the Addicks' First Team and those young players could have no better role model than Jason Euell.

Charlton Career:

Seasons: 2001/02 – 2005/06, 2011/12

Football League/Premier League: 102+48A 34G

FA Cup: 6+5A 3G

League Cup: 6+3A 2G

Football League Trophy: 0+1A 0G

Total: 114+57A 39G

2004/05   Shaun Bartlett

FA Premier League

Leading Scorer: Shaun Bartlett

Premier League:		25A	6G
FA Cup:		2A	2G
League Cup:		<u>0A</u>	<u>0G</u>
	Total	27A	8G

Shaun Bartlett
CHARLTON ATHLETIC FC

Thurston Shaun Bartlett

Born: Cape Town, South Africa, 31.10.1972

Career:
Cape Town Spurs* (116A 48G)
Colorado Rapids* (36A 9G)
Metrostars* (13A 2G)
Cape Town Spurs* (18A 8G)
FC Zurich* (77A 27G)
Charlton Athletic (PL 95+28A 24G)
Kaizer Chiefs* (31A 11G)
Bloemfontein Celtic* (8A 0G)
* Domestic league appearances including substitute appearances

Honours:
South Africa Full International – 74 caps-28 goals
(25 caps – 9 goals with Charlton)
African Cup of Nations winners' medal 1996 (with South Africa)
Swiss Cup winners' medal 2000 (with FC Zurich)
BBC - Premier League Goal of the Season 2000/01 (with Charlton)
Telkom Knockout Cup winners' medal 2007 (with Kaizer Chiefs)
MTN8 Cup winners' medal 2008 (with Kaizer Chiefs)

South African striker, Shaun Bartlett, commenced his career in his native Cape Town, playing at youth level for Norway Parks and Vasco Da Gama.

He signed as a professional for Cape Town Spurs in 1992 and won the first of his 74 international caps in 1995.

He moved to the USA in July 1995 to play in the MLS (Major League Soccer) for Colorado Rapids in Denver and New York Metrostars and, in 1996, he was part of the South Africa squad that won the African Cup of Nations.

In July 1997 he returned to Cape Town Spurs, initially on loan, and in July 1998 he moved continents again, signing for Swiss club FC Zurich. After a successful two years there, which included a Swiss Cup win and a run to the last 16 in the UEFA Cup – scoring 8 goals in his 8 appearances, he joined Charlton in December 2000 for a fee of £2m (=£3.3m).

Bartlett was a powerful striker with excellent aerial ability and, although he only played half of the 2000/01 season, his seven goals made him the Club's second highest scorer, behind Johansson with 14. His strike against Leicester City in April 2001, a superb volley, was selected as the Premier League's Goal of the Season.

The 2004/05 campaign was his fifth at The Valley and although he played in the opening two fixtures, he missed the next six through injury. He returned to the starting line-up in October, for the 1-1 home draw with Newcastle United, but did not score his first goals until November when he netted twice at White Hart Lane in a 3-2 victory over Tottenham Hotspur.

He really hit top form in January and February when he scored five goals in seven matches. It started with a strike against Birmingham City who were dispatched 3-1 in SE7, and he was then on target in the FA Cup fourth round tie at The Valley against Yeovil Town who were edged out 3-2.

He then gave the Addicks a first-half lead at home to Liverpool only for the visitors to come back and inflict a 1-2 defeat. In the FA Cup fifth round tie at home to Leicester City he netted the equaliser to make it 1-1 at half-time, but a last minute goal by the Foxes saw Charlton exit the competition 1-2.

His last goal of this sequence came in the next match at Middlesbrough which finished 2-2. His final goal of the season came in April at The Valley against Manchester City which also ended 2-2.

He missed another six games during the run-in but he returned for the final game, at home to Crystal Palace, which ended in another 2-2 stalemate, a result which relegated Palace.

Bartlett finished as top scorer with 8 goals, had he not missed 13 League matches he would surely have hit double figures. Charlton finished 11th, comfortably in mid-table.

Bartlett spent another season at The Valley before returning to South Africa in July 2006 to sign for Kaizer Chiefs in Johannesburg, before moving to Bloemfontain Celtic in July 2008 where he finished his playing career in 2009.

He has since forged a career in management in South Africa, starting as Assistant Manager with Golden Arrows in 2012, helping them to win the National First Division title in 2015. In 2016 he was appointed Manager of the University of Pretoria, leaving there in 2018 to become Assistant Manager at his old club, Kaizer Chiefs.

Shaun's playing career spanned three continents and he is South Africa's second most capped player with 74 appearances.

Charlton Career:

Seasons: 2000/01 – 2005/06

Premier League: 95+28A 24G

FA Cup: 10+2A 2G

League Cup: 4A 0G

Total: 109+30A 26G

2005/06   Darren Bent

FA Premier League

Leading Scorer: Darren Bent

Premier League:	36A	18G
FA Cup:	5A	2G
League Cup:	<u>2+1A</u>	<u>2G</u>
Total	43+1A	22G

Darren Bent
CHARLTON ATHLETIC FC

Darren Ashley Bent

Born: Tooting, London, 6.2.1984

Career:
Godmanchester Rovers
Ipswich Town (PL/FL 103+19A 49G)
Charlton Athletic (PL 68A 31G)
Tottenham Hotspur (PL 32+28A 18G)
Sunderland (PL 58A 32G)
Aston Villa (PL 45+16A 21G)
Fulham (loan) (PL 11+13A 3G)
Brighton & Hove Albion (loan) (FL 5A 2G)
Derby County (loan) (FL 11+4A 10G)
Derby County (FL 26+32A 12G)
Burton Albion (loan) (FL 10+5A 2G)

Honours:
England U15 – 8 caps –7 goals (with Ipswich Town)
England U16 –11 caps –3 goals (with Ipswich Town)
England U19 – 3 caps –3 goals (with Ipswich Town)
England U21 –14 caps –9 goals (with Ipswich Town)
England Full International – 13 caps – 4 goals (2 caps with Charlton)
Football League Cup winners' medal 2007/08 (with Tottenham)
Football League Cup runners-up medal 2008/09 (with Tottenham)

Darren Bent was spotted by Ipswich Town, while playing for Godmanchester Rovers in Cambridgeshire, and joined their youth system in 1998. He was signed as a professional in July 2001 and made his Premier League debut for them later that year.

He won England Youth and U21 honours while at Portman Road and gained a reputation as a prolific goal-scorer during his four seasons there. In June 2005, Charlton paid an initial fee of £2.5m to bring him to The Valley. That fee increased with add-ons to £5.175m (=£7.7m) which was, and still is, a Club record.

Bent made his Charlton debut in the opening match of the 2005/06 campaign at Sunderland, and he wasted no time in making his mark, scoring twice in a 3-1 victory. In fact he was on target in the opening four matches as he also scored at home to Wigan Athletic (1-0), away to Middlesbrough (3-0) and at Birmingham City (1-0). Five goals in his first four matches was an excellent start to his Addicks' career.

He was next on target in the League Cup second round tie at The Valley in September against Hartlepool United when the Addicks won 3-1. He then netted twice when Tottenham Hotspur visited SE7 in October, in a match where the hosts threw away a 2-0 lead to lose 2-3.

There was better news at Chelsea in the League Cup third round tie. Bent scored to level the scores at 1-1 and the match went to extra time and penalties, with Charlton winning the shoot-out 5-4.

Charlton's good early season form in the League then seemed to evaporate in November and they suffered five successive defeats. Bent scored in the last of these against Manchester City in a dismal 2-5 defeat in SE7. They did bounce back the following week and Bent scored in a 2-0 home victory over Sunderland.

The last match of the year saw another 2-0 victory at The Valley, this time against West Ham United, and Bent was again on target. That brought his goals total to 12.

In January he netted two more. First in the FA Cup third round tie at Sheffield Wednesday, where the Addicks triumphed 4-2, and then in the next match at home to Birmingham City who were edged out 2-0.

In February, Bent hit the net in three successive games starting with a 2-0 victory over Liverpool in SE7. He scored in a 2-3 defeat at Manchester City and then in the FA Cup fifth round at home to Brentford, who the Addicks eased past 3-1.

He had now netted 17 times and in March his form was recognised with his first Full England cap in a friendly against Uruguay. Later that month he hit a brace in a 2-1 home win over Middlesbrough and in the next home match he converted a penalty against Newcastle United in 3-1 victory.

In April, the Addicks managed only one win and that came at home to Portsmouth when Bent hit a late winner to take the points in a 2-1 victory. His next strike, and last of the season, came in the next match at Bolton Wanderers, but it was only a consolation as his penalty was the only bright spot in a 1-4 defeat.

Charlton finished in mid-table again, this time in 13th position.

Bent finished with 22 goals, 18 of which were scored in the Premier League, And it was no surprise when he was voted Charlton's Player of the Year.

Not only was he Charlton's top scorer but he was also the highest scoring Englishman in the Premier League, and was runner-up to Wayne Rooney in the PFA Young Player of the Year award. All of which made it hard to understand why he was not included in England's World Cup squad in May 2006.

Charlton Career:

See Season 2006/07

2006/07 Darren Bent

FA Premier League

Leading Scorer: Darren Bent

Premier League:	32A	13G
FA Cup:	0A	0G
League Cup:	2+1A	2G
	Total 34+1A	15G

Darren Bent
CHARLTON ATHLETIC FC

Alan Curbishley's decision to leave the Club in May 2006 resulted in a seismic change in the Addicks' fortunes, He had been manager, or joint manager, for 15 years and had masterminded promotions to the Premier League in 1998 and 2000.

His replacement was Iain Dowie who had recently left Crystal Palace. Among his new signings was Jimmy Floyd-Hasselbaink from Chelsea to partner Darren Bent up front.

Charlton made a disastrous start to the 2006/07 campaign. The first match was at West Ham United and despite Bent giving the visitors a first-half lead by converting a penalty, the Addicks unraveled in the second-half and slumped to a 1-3 defeat.

The next match was also lost but then came the first win as Bent netted twice, once from the spot, to defeat Bolton Wanderers 2-0 at The Valley.

However, it did not herald a revival as the next five League games all ended in defeat. One bright moment during this run was in the League Cup second round at home to Carlisle United, where Bent netted the only goal in a 1-0 victory. He also scored in the home defeat to Arsenal (1-2) and at Fulham (1-2) which left the Addicks with seven defeats in their opening eight League matches.

The second League win of the season did not arrive until November when Bent provided the decisive strike to defeat Manchester City 1-0 in SE7. He was also on target in the next match which was in the League Cup fourth round at Chesterfield. The match finished 3-3, after extra time, with Bent scoring once to supplement two from Hasselbaink, and the Addicks went on to win 4-3 on penalties. Bent also netted a penalty in the shoot-out.

The 2-3 defeat at Wigan Athletic in the next match signaled the end of Dowie's tenure as manager. He had overseen just two wins in the opening 12 League matches. His assistant, Les Reed, was drafted into the hot-seat.

Results did not improve, however, and Reed only managed one win in eight matches, which included is dismal 0-1 home defeat to Wycombe Wanderers in the Quarter-final of the League Cup. The axe fell on Christmas Eve and former Addicks player, Alan Pardew, became the Club's third manager of the season.

There was an immediate reaction. Bent was on target in Pardew's first match in charge as the Addicks drew 2-2 with Fulham at The Valley, a match in which they were cruelly denied three points by a last minute equaliser from the visitors. A victory was achieved three days later though and Bent was again on target in a 2-1 home win over Aston Villa.

However, the next six matches brought only one win, all of which Bent missed through injury, but there was a glimmer of hope in February when the Addicks went on a six match unbeaten run. It started with a 4-0 mauling of West Ham United (managed by Alan Curbishley) in SE7 with Bent among the scorers. He also netted a late penalty against Wigan Athletic to secure a 1-0 home win in March.

Having given themselves some hope of survival, the Addicks then failed to win any of their final five matches. Bent did score at Everton (1-2) and at Blackburn Rovers (1-4) but the inevitable relegation was confirmed in the penultimate match, a 0-2 defeat to Tottenham Hotspur at The Valley.

With their fate sealed, Charlton travelled to Liverpool for their last match and almost pulled off an unlikely victory. Bent scored in the 2-2 draw with the hosts only equalising in the last minute.

He finished the season with 15 goals but could not prevent the Addicks finishing in 19th position which brought their seven season stay in the Premier League to an end.

There was no way that Charlton could hang onto their talisman striker and Bent joined Tottenham Hotspur in June 2007 for a fee of £16.5m (=£23m) which was, and still is, a Charlton record for an outgoing transfer.

His Premier League career continued with Spurs before moving to Sunderland in August 2009 for an initial £10m fee, which rose to £16.5m (=£22.3m). Aston Villa were the next beneficiaries of his talents when he signed for them in January 2011 for a fee of £18m, which rose to £24m (=£29.5m).

A loan spell with Fulham in September 2013 preceded loan moves to Brighton & Hove Albion in November 2014 and Derby County in January 2015. He joined the Rams permanently later that year and stayed with them for three years, during which he also spent a loan spell with Burton Albion in January 2018.

Darren Bent retired in July 2018 having enjoyed a magnificent career for club and country. His League career totaled 486 matches and he netted 180 goals.

He was immensely popular at The Valley and was undoubtedly one of the best strikers in the Club's history.

Darren is now working for the BBC as a football pundit.

Charlton Career:

Seasons: 2005/06 – 2006/07

Premier League: 68A 31G

FA Cup: 5A 2G

League Cup: 4+2A 4G

Total: 77+2A 37G

2007/08 Chris Iwelumo

Football League – Championship

Leading Scorer: Chris Iwelumo

Football League:	32+14A	10G
FA Cup:	0+2A	0G
League Cup:	0+2A	0G
Total	32+18A	10G

Chris Iwelumo
CHARLTON ATHLETIC FC

Christopher Robert Iwelumo

Born: Coatbridge, Scotland, 1.8.1978

Career:
St Mirren (SL 9+22A 1G)
Aarhus Fremad (Denmark)* (27A 4G)
Stoke City (FL 40+44A 16G)
York City (loan) (FL 11+1A 2G)
Cheltenham Town (loan) (FL 2+2A 1G)
Brighton & Hove Albion (loan) (FL 10A 4G)
Alemannia Aachen (Germany)* (0+9A 0G)
Colchester United (FL 87+5A 35G)
Charlton Athletic (FL 32+14A 10G)
Wolverhampton Wanderers (FL/PL 27+19A 14G)
Bristol City (loan) (FL 7A 2G)
Burnley (FL 29+16A 11G)
Watford (FL 25+21A 4G)
Notts County (loan) (FL 5A 0G)
Oldham Athletic (loan) (FL 4+3A 1G)
Scunthorpe United (FL 4+8A 2G)
St Johnstone (SL 0+6A 0G)
Chester (Conference 10A 1G)
(* record in domestic league including substitute appearances)

Honours:

Scotland 'B' International – 1 cap (with Charlton)
Scotland Full International – 4 caps (with Wolverhampton W.)
Football League Trophy winners' medal 2000 (with Stoke City)
FL Second Division (Tier 3) Play-off winners' medal 2001/02
(with Stoke City)
FL Second Division (Tier 3) Play-off winners' medal 2003/04
(with Brighton)
FL League One (Tier 3) runners-up 2005/06 (with Colchester)
FL Championship (Tier 2) Champions medal 2008/09
(with Wolverhampton W.)
Scottish FA Cup winners' medal 2013/14 (with St Johnstone)

Scottish striker Chris Iwelumo came through the youth system at St Mirren, who he joined in 1995, and signed as a professional in 1996.

After three seasons playing in the Scottish League, he moved to Danish club Aarhus Fremad in 1998 but after two seasons he returned to the UK to sign for Stoke City in March 2000, the Potters paying a fee of £180,000 (=£305,000). He helped Stoke win the Football League Trophy in 2000 and promotion to the First Division (Tier 2) in 2002 via the Play-offs.

While at Stoke he had a number of loan spells at York City, Cheltenham Town and Brighton & Hove Albion, where he helped the Seagulls win promotion to the First Division (Tier 2) with another Play-off Final win in 2004.

He then moved abroad again, this time to Germany, where he joined Alemannia Aachen but after only one season he returned to England to sign for Colchester United in July 2005. His career blossomed with the Essex club and he was a key component in the team which finished runners-up in League One (Tier 3) and gained promotion to the Championship in 2006.

His goal-scoring exploits attracted the attention of Charlton who had been relegated from the Premier League in 2007 and were looking for a replacement for the departed Darren Bent. Iwelumo, was out of contact at

Colchester so no fee was involved when he signed for the Addicks in July 2007 hoping to spearhead a quick return to the top tier.

A tall powerful striker, he opened his account in the third match, at home to Sheffield Wednesday, where he netted twice as the Addicks came back from 0-2 down to win 3-2. Further goals followed against Leicester City in a 2-0 Valley victory in September, and at Hull City in October where the Addicks secured a 2-1 win.

In November, Iwelumo was on target in three successive matches. The sequence started with a last minute winner at Southampton (1-0) and he replicated that in the next match at Bristol City when his 90th minute strike again clinched a 1-0 victory. Next up were Cardiff City in SE7 and he added another goal to his total as the Addicks eased to a 3-0 win.

His form brought him international recognition. He was actually qualified to play for two countries, as he has a Nigerian father and a Scottish mother, but it was Scotland he opted for and he was selected for the Scotland 'B' team in November for their match against the Republic of Ireland, which ended 1-1.

He brought his tally up to nine in December by scoring against Ipswich Town at The Valley (3-1) and at West Bromwich Albion (2-4), and Charlton were well placed in the League at the turn of the year.

However, the second half of the season saw the Addicks promotion hopes gradually evaporate as they gained only six wins in their last 23 matches. Iwelumo was mainly used as a substitute, coming off the bench 12 times during this period, and he only added one more goal. It came in March in a 2-0 victory at Sheffield United.

Charlton finished in a disappointing 11th position, six points away from even the Play-off places, so there was no instant return to the Premier League.

Iwelumo was top scorer with 10 goals and he figured in all 46 League games, 14 of them as substitute.

In July 2008 Wolverhampton Wanderers came in with a bid for the striker and he moved to Molineux for a fee of £468,000 (=£630,000). It was money well spent as he helped them to win the Championship title in 2009 and promotion to the Premier League. It was during his time at Wolves that he gained Full international honours for Scotland, winning four caps.

After a loan spell at Bristol City in February 2010, Iwelumo made a permanent move to Burnley in July 2010. The Clarets paid a fee of £428,000 (=£550,000), but after only one season at Turf Moor he was on his travels again, Watford signed him in July 2011 for a £315,000 (=£386,000) fee.

Two more loan spells followed at Notts County and Oldham Athletic before he made a permanent move to Scunthorpe United in July 2013. Just six months later he returned to Scotland to sign for St Johnstone and he gained a Scottish Cup winners' medal with them in 2014, being an unused substitute in the final.

In June 2014 he joined his final club, Chester, in the Football Conference. He played ten matches for them, scoring once before hanging up is boots in October 2014.

Chris Iwelumo enjoyed a nomadic career, paying for 18 clubs and scoring 108 goals in the various leagues. After retirement he went to university and obtained a degree in journalism and he now works in the media as a football pundit on TV and radio.

Charlton Career:

Seasons: 2007/08

Football League: 32+14A   10G

FA Cup: 0+2A   0G

League Cup: 0+2A   0G

Total: 32+18A   10G

2008/09   Nicky Bailey

Football League – Championship

Leading Scorer: Nicky Bailey

Football League:	43A	13G
FA Cup:	3A	0G
League Cup:	0A	0G
Total	46A	13G

Nicholas Francis Bailey

Born: Putney, London, 10.6.1984

Career:
Fulham
Sutton United
Barnet (FL 88+1A 12G)
Southend United (FL 43+2A 9G)
Charlton Athletic (FL 86+1A 25G)
Middlesbrough (FL 84+15A 4G)
Millwall (FL 31+5A 1G)
Barnet (FL 1+1A 0G)
Sutton United
Havant & Waterlooville

Honours:
England 'C' International (Semi-pro) – 4 caps (with Barnet)
Conference National champions medal 2004/05 (with Barnet)
National League South champions medal 2015/16 (with Sutton)

Midfielder Nicky Bailey developed in Fulham's youth academy. He was released in 2000 and joined Sutton United where he gained a reputation as a goal-scoring midfielder with an excellent range of passing.

Barnet, then in the Football Conference, paid £10,000 (=£15,500) for his services in June 2004 and he helped them to win the Conference title and promotion to the Football League in 2005. While at Barnet he was capped four times for the England 'C' team and he was voted the Bees' Player of the Year in 2006.

In August 2007, Southend United paid £175,000 (=£245,000) to take him to

Roots Hall where he was top scorer and Player of the Year in his first season, 2007/08.

Charlton moved to sign him in August 2008, paying a fee of £750,000 (=£1m) as they embarked on their second season back in the Championship. It turned out to be a disappointing season for the Addicks but Bailey was one of the few positives in a disastrous campaign.

The season started well enough with two wins in the opening three fixtures, Bailey scored his first goal for the Club in September at home to Wolverhampton Wanderers. His early strike gave the Addicks a half-time lead but Wolves hit back with three second-half goals to inflict a 1-3 defeat which seemed to set the tone for the season.

In October he was on target at The Valley again as Ipswich Town were edged out 2-1, which was only the fourth win of the season. He netted at Ipswich later in the month too to secure a 1-1 draw but Charlton were by now struggling at the bottom of the table.

In November, the axe finally fell on manager Alan Pardew after a dismal 2-5 home defeat to Sheffield United. Only four games had been won out of 18. Pardew's assistant, Phil Parkinson, was installed as caretaker manager.

Results did not improve, however, and that win against Ipswich in October was followed by an 18 match winless run which included 12 defeats. Bailey did provide some hope when he scored a brace against Queens Park Rangers on Boxing Day in SE7 to secure a 2-2 draw.

The winless run was finally ended in January with a 1-0 home victory over Crystal Palace and Bailey scored his sixth of the season in the next match at Burnley, but it was not enough to avoid a 1-2 defeat.

In February the Addicks managed a rare win on Valentine's Day at The Valley against Plymouth Argyle. Bailey was on target in the 2-0 victory. He then scored in successive games at Swansea City (1-1) and at home to Doncaster Rovers (1-2).

A goal at Reading in a 2-2 draw in March brought his total to ten and he was also on target in a rare away win at Southampton in April where the Addicks triumphed 3-2. It was all too little, too late, however as three matches later relegation was confirmed following a 2-2 home draw with Blackpool.

Bailey did mange two more goals in the home matches with Cardiff City (2-2) and in the final game with Norwich City, who were also relegated. Bailey opened the scoring and Deon Burton netted a hat-trick in the 4-2 victory.

Charlton finished bottom of the table in 24th position and only two years after being in the Premier League, they found themselves in the third tier of English football.

Despite this, Bailey had a successful season finishing as top-scorer with 13 goals and being voted Player of the Year for the third time in his career.

Despite relegation, Bailey stayed at The Valley for the 2009/10 campaign as the Addicks looked to achieve an immediate return to the Championship. In the event they came pretty close, finishing fourth and qualifying for the Play-offs. Bailey had another successful season and again netted 13 goals.

Swindon Town stood in their way in the semi-final and, with each club winning their home leg 2-1, they were level 3-3 on aggregate. The tie had to be decided on penalties at The Valley but the Addicks lost 4-5, with Bailey uncharacteristically missing the crucial spot kick.

With their promotion hopes dashed, it was to prove impossible for Charlton to retain the services of their talented midfielder. In July 2010, Middlesbrough paid a fee of £1.4m (=£1.8m) for him and he was able to continue his career in the Championship. At Boro he was deployed in a deeper midfield role and made over 100 appearances.

After three years at The Riverside Stadium, Bailey returned to London to sign for Millwall in August 2013. He was plagued by injuries for much of his two years with the Lions and he left the club following their relegation to League One in 2015.

In October 2015, he returned to one of his old clubs, Barnet, who had just regained their place in the Football League. However, his stay was brief and he left the Bees in December 2015 to rejoin another of his old clubs, Sutton United.

Bailey enjoyed a successful three and a half years with Sutton, which included winning the National League South title in 2015/16 and a historic run to the 5th round of the FA Cup in 2016/17, before departing at the end of the 2018/19 campaign.

The 2019/20 season saw Nicky Bailey still in action in the National League South for Havant & Waterlooville, helping them to finish in second position and reach the Play-offs, where they lost to Dartford in the semi-final.

Charlton Career:

Seasons: 2008/09 – 2009/10

Football League: 86+1A 25G

FA Cup: 4A 0G

League Cup: 0+1A 0G

Football League Trophy: 1A 1G

Play-Offs: 2A 0G

Total: 93+2A 26G

2009/10   Deon Burton

Football League – League One

Leading Scorer: Deon Burton

Football League:	35+4A	13G
FA Cup:	0+1A	0G
League Cup:	0+1A	0G
Football League Trophy	0+1A	0G
Play-offs:	2A	1G
Total	37+7A	14G

Deon Burton
CHARLTON ATHLETIC FC

Deon John Burton

Born: Reading, Berkshire, 25.10.1976

Career:
Portsmouth (FL 42+20A 10G)
Cardiff City (loan) (FL 5A 2G)
Derby County (PL/FL 78+47A 25G)
Barnsley (loan) (FL 3A 0G)
Stoke City (loan) (FL 11+1A 2G)
Portsmouth (loan) (FL 6A 3G)
Portsmouth (FL/PL 5+5A 1G)
Walsall (loan) (FL 2+1A 0G)
Swindon Town (loan) (FL 4A 1G)
Brentford (FL 38+2A 10G)
Rotherham United (FL 24A 12G)
Sheffield Wednesday (FL 82+34A 23G)
Charlton Athletic (FL 47+12A 18G)
Gabala (Azerbaijan)
Gillingham (FL 31+9A 12G)
Scunthorpe United (FL 20+14A 6G)
York City (loan) (FL 1A 0G)
Eastleigh
Brackley Town
Worcester City

Honours:

Jamaica Full International – 60 caps – 9 goals (1 cap with Charlton)

Jamaican Sportsman of the Year 1997

FL Second Division (Tier 3) Play-off winners' medal 2001/02 (with Stoke City)

FL First Division (Tier 2) champions medal 2002/03 (with Portsmouth)

FL League Two (Tier 4) champions medal 2012/13 (with Gillingham)

FL League Two (Tier 4) runners-up 2013/14 (with Scunthorpe Utd)

Born in Reading, Deon Burton started his career with Portsmouth and made his League debut in the 1993/94 season. He spent three years with Pompey, during which he spent a loan spell with Cardiff City in December 1996, before moving to Premier League side Derby County for a £1m fee (=£1.8m) in August 1997.

He spent five years with Derby during which he gained the first of his 60 international caps for Jamaica. He also had loan spells at Barnsley, Stoke City – where he won the Second Division (Tier 3) Play-offs in 2002 - and Portsmouth in August 2002. In December 2002 he rejoined Portsmouth on a permanent basis, with Pompey paying a fee of £250,000 (=£410,000) and he helped them to win promotion to the Premier League in 2003 by winning the First Division title.

There were then further loan spells with Walsall and Swindon Town before he made a permanent move to Brentford in August 2004. After netting 10 League goals in his first season, he moved to Rotherham United in July 2005 where his 14 goals in only 27 League and cup matches prompted Sheffield Wednesday to pay £110,000 (=£160,000) for his services in January 2006.

He stayed at Hillsborough for nearly three years, racking up 124 appearances and netting 25 goals, before joining Charlton in November 2008. He scored five goals for the Addicks that season but could not prevent the Club suffering relegation from the Championship.

Charlton were the 11th club of Burton's nomadic career and it was hoped that his experience and goals would fire the Addicks straight back to the Championship in 2009/10. As it turned out he came pretty close to doing so.

Burton opened his account in the second League match at Hartlepool United where the Addicks triumphed 2-0. Nicky Bailey scored the second goal and the pair were to be the Club's main source of goals throughout the campaign. Burton was also on target in the next match, at home to Leyton Orient, which brought another victory (2-1).

The Addicks made a great start to the season, winning all six of their opening League matches. The sixth victory was at home to Brentford, with Burton notching his third of the season in the 2-0 win. The next two fixtures were drawn but Burton was on target in both, at home to Southampton (1-1) and at Norwich City (2-2).

Charlton did not suffer defeat in the League until the end of September, at Colchester United (0-3), and they were still well placed in the table when they lost their second match a month later at Carlisle United (1-3), Burton's penalty being their only consolation.

His next strike came in happier circumstances when he added the fifth goal at The Valley as MK Dons were thrashed 5-1 in November. The next home match was also high scoring with the Addicks easing past Bristol Rovers 4-2 with the aid of a Burton penalty. This started a four match winning run and Burton hit the net in two of the victories, at Brighton & Hove Albion (2-0) and at home to Southend United (1-0).

In December, the local derby with Millwall in SE7 ended in an eye-catching 4-4 draw. Burton contributed two penalties in the eight goal thriller. That brought his total to 12 goals and his 13th came in February in a 1-1 draw at Walsall.

He did not score in the remaining League matches but the Addicks finished in fourth place and qualified for the Play-offs. They had to play Swindon Town in the semi-final and the first-leg was at the County Ground. Swindon stormed into a two lead but a late goal from Burton reduced the deficit to 1-2 and gave the Addicks hope of turning things round at The Valley.

Charlton won the second-leg 2-1 which tied the aggregate score at 3-3 so the match went to penalties. Unfortunately it was Swindon who edged through, as the Addicks lost 4-5 on spot kicks.

Burton finished top-scorer with 14 goals as the Addicks came so close to achieving their objective.

He left the Club at the end of the season and signed for Azerbaijan Premier League club Gabala, who were managed by former Arsenal and England captain, Tony Adams. He spent two seasons there before returning to England in August 2012 to sign for Gillingham.

In his first season with the Kent club, Burton helped them to win the League Two championship (Tier 4) in 2013. But he was then on the move again in July 2013 to Scunthorpe United where he also won promotion from League Two in 2014 as the Iron finished as runners-up.

In October 2014 he joined York City on loan and they became his 15th club and his last in the Football League.

That was not the end of his senior career however, as in 2015 he signed for Eastleigh of the Football Conference – now the National League (Tier 5) and subsequently played in the National League North for Brackley Town and Worcester City. He finally retired in July 2016, just four months short of his 40th birthday.

Deon Burton represented 18 clubs during his 22 year career. He played in 544 matches in the Football League and Premier League and netted 125 goals. He is now disseminating that experience by running his own Football Training Academy and coaching the U23 squad at West Bromwich Albion.

Charlton Career:

Seasons: 2008/09 – 2009/10

Football League: 47+12A 18G

FA Cup: 3+1A 0G

League Cup: 0+1A 0G

Football League Trophy: 0+1A 0G

Play-Offs: 2A 1G

Total: 52+15A 19G

2010/11 Johnnie Jackson

Football League – League One

Leading Scorer: Johnnie Jackson

Football League:	29+1A	13G
FA Cup:	5A	1G
League Cup:	0A	0G
Football League Trophy	2+1A	0G
Total	36+2A	14G

Johnnie Jackson
CHARLTON ATHLETIC FC

John Alec Jackson

Born: Camden, London 15.8.1982

Career:
Tottenham Hotspur (PL 12+8A 1G)
Swindon Town (loan) (FL 12+1A 1G)
Colchester United (loan) (FL 8A 0G)
Coventry City (loan) (FL 2+3A 2G)
Watford (loan) (FL 14+1A 0G)
Derby County (loan) (FL 3+3A 0G)
Colchester United (FL 92+15A 13G)
Notts County (FL 20+4A 2G)
Charlton Athletic (loan) (FL 4A 0G)
Charlton Athletic (FL 211+32A 51G)

Honours:
England U17 – 1 cap (with Tottenham Hotspur)
England U18 – 8 caps (with Tottenham Hotspur)
England U20 – 6 caps (with Tottenham Hotspur)
FL League Two (Tier 4) champions medal 2010 (with Notts County)
FL League One (Tier 3) champions medal 2012 (with Charlton)

Midfielder Johnnie Jackson came through the youth system at Tottenham Hotspur and signed professional in March 2000. He eventually made his Premier League debut for Spurs in December 2003 and scored his first goal in February 2004, ironically against Charlton at The Valley.

During his time at White Hart Lane he spent loan spells at Swindon Town, Colchester United, Coventry City, Watford and Derby County. He was released by Spurs in the summer of 2006 and signed for Colchester United, who were then in the Championship, and he enjoyed a three year spell there, making over 100 appearances and being voted their Player of the Year in 2008.

In August 2009, Notts County signed Jackson for an undisclosed fee and in his first season at Meadow Lane (2009/10) they finished as Champions of League Two.

Equally at home at left-back or left-midfield, he initially joined the Addicks on loan in February 2010, playing in four matches at left-back. He obviously impressed, as he joined Charlton on a permanent basis in July 2010 and he went on to become one of the Club's most significant signings.

As the Addicks embarked on their second season in League One in 2010/11, Jackson became the regular left-back. He scored his first goal for the Club in September at home to Dagenham & Redbridge, netting in the 90th minute to secure a 2-2 draw.

He then began to be used regularly in midfield where his talents was used to greater effect. In October he was on target in a 4-3 victory at Carlisle United and in November he netted in three successive games, all of which were won. It started with a goal at Swindon Town in a 3-0 victory and he then hit a brace, one a penalty, at Peterborough United as the Addicks dished out a 5-1 thrashing. He replicated that at home to Yeovil Town who were edged out 3-2, with Jackson scoring twice again, once from the spot.

He also scored in the FA Cup second round tie at The Valley where the Addicks were held 2-2 by Luton Town, although they won replay 3-1.

His stellar performances were rewarded by being voted the League One Player of the Month for November.

At the end of December he converted another penalty at Brighton & Hove Albion in a 1-1 draw, and that started another "goal-den" sequence as he was also on target in the next three matches.

On New Year's Day, Charlton fought out a 3-3 draw at Colchester United with Jackson netting two spot-kicks. He then scored at The Valley but the Addicks slumped to a 2-4 defeat at the hands of Swindon Town – a result which cost manager Phil Parkinson his job. Another spot-kick at Sheffield Wednesday helped to secure a point in a 2-2 draw, although the Addicks threw away a 2-0 lead. Chris Powell was then appointed manager and started with four straight wins, raising hopes of another push for promotion.

Jackson's total now stood at 13 goals and in February he scored what turned out to be his last goal of the season as Charlton eased past Peterborough United 3-2 in SE7. He played in only three more matches as he suffered a serious achilles injury at Notts County at the end of February, which effectively finished his season as he missed the last 16 matches.

After the Peterborough victory in Powell's fourth game, Charlton's form dipped alarmingly and they managed only two wins in the last 19 matches, slipping to a disappointing 13th position.

Jackson finished as top scorer with 14 goals despite playing 11 League games at left-back and missing the last 16 matches through injury. His tally would have been so much higher had his season not been terminated so early. His absence also had a significant effect on Charlton's fortunes too.

The fans recognised his contribution as he finished as runner-up, to Jose Semedo, in the Player of the Year poll.

Charlton Career:

See Season 2012/13

2011/12   Bradley Wright-Phillips

Football League – League One

Leading Scorer: Bradley Wright-Phillips

Football League:	41+1A	22G
FA Cup:	1+2A	0G
League Cup:	0A	0G
Football League Trophy:	0A	0G
Total	42+3A	22G

Bradley Wright-Phillips
CHARLTON ATHLETIC FC

Bradley Edward Wright-Phillips

Born: Lewisham, London, 12.3.1985

Career:
Manchester City (PL 1+31A 2G)
Southampton (FL 58+53A 22G)
Plymouth Argyle (FL 29+3A 17G)
Charlton Athletic (FL 71+11A 32G)
Brentford (loan) (FL 10+5A 5G)
New York Red Bulls (MLS)
Los Angeles FC (MLS)

Honours:
England U20 – 5 caps (with Manchester City)
FL League One (Tier 3) champions medal 2011/12 (with Charlton)
Major League Soccer Golden Boot 2014 (with New York Red Bulls)
Major League Soccer Golden Boot 2016 (with New York Red Bulls)

Bradley Wright-Phillips is a graduate of Manchester City's youth academy and signed professional for them in July 2002.

He comes from a footballing family as he is the son of former Arsenal and England star, Ian Wright, and the half-brother of Shaun Wright-Phillips (Manchester City, Chelsea, QPR and England).

He scored on his Premier League debut for City in December 2004 but the majority of his appearances were from the bench and he moved to Southampton in July 2006 in search of regular first team football. The Saints parted with £500,000 (=£730,000) to secure his services.

A pacey striker, Wright-Phillips established himself as a predatory finisher in the Championship and stayed at Southampton for three years. Their relegation to League One in May 2009 saw him released from his contract and he signed for Plymouth Argyle where he continued to score regularly in the Championship.

During his time at Home Park, he was troubled by a persistent knee injury (patella tendonitis) and he subsequently had to manage this condition throughout his career.

In January 2011, he became Chris Powell's first signing for Charlton, the Addicks paying an undisclosed fee. It proved to be a shrewd piece of business by Powell, as Wright-Phillips scored in each of his first three games and finished the season with nine strikes from only 20 starts in League One.

The 2011/12 campaign proved to be hugely successful for Charlton and Wright-Phillips. Powell had radically overhauled the squad in a bid to mount a promotion challenge and they started well, winning the first two matches.

Wright-Phillips opened his account in the third match as he scored twice at Colchester United to secure a 2-0 victory. He was on target in the next match too, netting once at The Valley as the Addicks were held 2-2 by Scunthorpe United.

In September, he scored in successive home matches against Sheffield Wednesday (1-1) and Exeter City (2-0) as the undefeated Addicks topped the League One table. His sixth goal came in the next home match as Chesterfield were eased past 3-1.

By this time he was playing up front with French striker Yann Kermorgant and the pair went on to develop a prolific partnership.

At the beginning of October, they both scored as Sheffield United were dispatched 2-0 in SE7 and it was not until the 13th match that the Addicks tasted defeat, going down 0-1 at Stevenage.

That proved to be just a blip as Charlton won the next six matches and Wright-Phillips was on target in five of them, hitting seven goals in the process. The sequence started at home to Carlisle United who were thumped 4-0 and he then scored a brace at Wycombe Wanderers in a 2-1 victory. Another double came at Hartlepool United in a 4-0 mauling before he netted once back at The Valley where Preston North End were totally eclipsed 5-2. He rounded off his scoring spree by scoring the only goal at Brentford to secure a 1-0 triumph.

His total now stood at 14 goals and, although the Addicks suffered their second defeat of the season on New Year's Eve at Leyton Orient (0-1), they then put an 11 match unbeaten run together to further cement their position at the top of the table.

Wright-Phillips experienced a lean period in front of goal despite the positive results and did not score again until February when his strike helped to gain revenge on Stevenage who were beaten 2-0 at The Valley. Three days later he was really back on form as he netted a hat-trick at Chesterfield, who were thrashed 4-0.

In March he was on target in three successive matches, although the first strike came in an unexpected 2-4 home defeat to Notts County. An early goal at Scunthorpe United helped to secure a point (1-1) before he hit his 21st goal of the season at home to Yeovil Town who were defeated 3-0.

Into April and the Addicks only needed a win at Carlisle United to clinch promotion. They did just that and appropriately it was Wright-Phillips who scored the goal to secure a 1-0 victory and a return to the Championship for Charlton after a three year absence. A week later they were confirmed as Champions following a 2-1 victory over Wycombe Wanderers at The Valley.

Wright-Phillips finished as top scorer with 22 goals, the best total by a Charlton player since Darren Bent's 22 strikes in 2005/06.

Charlton finished as Champions with a record 101 points, but that would not have been achieved without Bradley Wright-Phillips' lethal finishing.

Back in the Championship for the 2012/13 campaign, Wright-Phillips was a regular starter up front until October when he began to struggle for fitness with his knee injury. He was mainly used from the bench after that and, having lost his regular place, he went on loan to Brentford in February 2013 where he netted five times in only ten starts.

At the end of the season he left The Valley and signed for New York Red Bulls in July 2013. He had great success playing in the MLS and in his first season he scored 27 goals to set a new club record. He twice won the MLS Golden Boot (2014 & 2016) and is the Bulls record goal-scorer having netted 126 goals in his 240 appearances.

In February 2020, he moved to Los Angeles FC to continue his MLS career.

Bradley will always be remembered in a corner of South-East London for the goals he scored to secure that League One Championship with a record number of points.

Charlton Career:

Seasons: 2010/11 – 2012/13

Football League: 71+11A 32G

FA Cup: 2+2A 0G

League Cup: 0+1A 0G

Total: 73+14A 32G

2012/13   Johnnie Jackson

Football League – Championship

Leading Scorer: Johnnie Jackson

Football League:	41+2A	12G
FA Cup:	0+1A	0G
League Cup:	0+1A	0G
Total	41+4A	12G

Johnnie Jackson
CHARLTON ATHLETIC FC

Having captained Charlton to the League One title in the previous campaign, Johnnie Jackson played a pivotal role in establishing them in the Championship in 2012/13.

He was moved from left-side midfield to a more central role and scored a number of crucial goals throughout the season.

The Addicks made a slow start, only winning once in their opening six matches, but Jackson opened his account for the season in the seventh game when he scored the opener at Ipswich Town which set up a 2-1 victory. A week later he was on target at The Valley against Blackburn Rovers in a 1-1 draw.

Going into November, the Addicks were still struggling for consistent form when Cardiff City came to SE7 on a Tuesday evening. The visitors took control of the match and the Addicks were 0-2 down heading into half-time. Jackson then turned the game on its head, scoring twice before the interval to level things up at 2-2. The second-half produced another five goals and Charlton netted three of them to eventually edge home 5-4.

By the half-way point of the season, Jackson had four goals to his name but he was to go on to treble that by the end of the campaign.

His next strike came on New Year's Day at Watford in another high-scoring encounter. Charlton won 4-3 and it was Jackson who scored the late winner. He was on target in the next home League game too as Blackpool were defeated 2-1. He rounded January off with another goal at Sheffield Wednesday but two late strikes from the Owls inflicted a 1-2 defeat.

In March, Jackson hit his eighth goal in the 2-2 draw at Peterborough United and he really hit form in the last eight matches of the season, in which the Addicks were unbeaten, when he was on target in four of those games.

The sequence started at The Valley against Bolton Wanderers who took a two goal lead. Jackson scored to get Charlton back into the game and they eventually prevailed 3-2. The next home game saw Leeds United visit SE7 and Jackson netted the opening goal in a match where the hosts triumphed

2-1 thanks to a last minute winner from Jonathan Obika.

A week later the Addicks were in action at Barnsley and an incredible afternoon unfolded. Charlton set a new Club record with a 6-0 away win and Jackson was one of the six goal-scorers.

In the last match, Charlton hosted Bristol City and rounded off the campaign with an emphatic 4-1 victory. Fittingly it was Jackson who netted the fourth and final goal of the season.

Charlton finished in ninth position to consolidate their place in the Championship.

Jackson was top scorer with 12 goals, the third successive season that he had reached double figures. He was also runner-up to Chris Solly in the Player of the Year poll.

Jackson continued as Charlton's captain for the next five years and moved to a player/coach role for the 2017/18 campaign. He retired at the end of that season having amassed 499 career appearances, which included 279 for the Addicks.

He was appointed Assistant Manager to Lee Bowyer for 2018/19 and helped to mastermind the third place finish in League One and eventual promotion to the Championship, via the dramatic 2-1 victory over Sunderland at Wembley.

Johnnie is still Assistant Manager and remains a firm fans favourite. It is just a matter of time before he too is inducted into the Charlton Hall of Fame in recognition of his outstanding contribution to the Club both on and off the field.

Charlton Career:

Seasons: 2009/10, 2010/11 – 2017/18

Football League: 215+32A 51G

FA Cup: 16+1A 3G

League Cup: 6+1A 0G

Football League Trophy: 6+2A 0G

Total: 243+36A 54G*

* Given as 55 goals by some sources but analysis of each season's matches confirms his total as 54 goals (51 League + 3 FA Cup).

2013/14   Yann Kermorgant & Marvin Sordell

Football League – Championship
Leading Scorers: Yann Kermorgant & Marvin Sordell

Yann Kermorgant

Football League:	17+4A	5G
FA Cup:	2A	3G
League Cup:	0+1A	0G
Total	19+5A	8G

Yann Kermorgant
CHARLTON ATHLETIC FC

Yann Alain Kermorgant

Born: Vannes, Brittany, France, 8.11.1981

Career:
Vannes
Chatellerault
Grenoble
Stade Reims
Leicester City (FL 9+11A 1G)
Arles-Avignon (loan)
Charlton Athletic (FL 78+11A 28G)
AFC Bournemouth (FL/PL 37+24A 24G)
Reading (FL 63+23A 23G)
Vannes

Honours:
FL League One (Tier 3) Champions medal 2011/12 (with Charlton)
FL Championship (Tier 2) Champions medal 2014/15 (with AFC Bournemouth)
Brittany v Mali (May 2013) – scoring the only goal in a 1-0 win.

French striker Yann Kermorgant commenced his career with his home town club Vannes, in the fourth tier of French football in 2002 by which time he was 20. His career had been halted for four years as he was diagnosed with leukemia at the age of fourteen.

He moved to Chatellerault in 2004 before moving up to tier 2, signing for Grenoble (2005) and Stade Reims (2007). His scoring record in the French League attracted the attention of Leicester City, then in the Championship, and following a trial he was signed by the Foxes in August 2009.

After one season, he went on loan to French tier 1 club Arles-Avignon where he spent the 2010/11 season. At the end of his loan Leicester City allowed him to look for another club and Charlton were the beneficiaries.

Chris Powell knew the Frenchman from his days as first team coach at Leicester and signed him in September 2011. It was a significant signing as Kermorgant went on to become one of the most popular players in Charlton's recent history.

He made an immediate impact, forming a productive partnership with fellow striker Bradley Wright-Phillips as the Addicks romped to the League One title in 2012 with a record number of points (101).

Kermorgant netted 12 goals that season but it was his all-round contribution that won the hearts of the fans. He possessed great aerial ability and was also a dead-ball specialist, scoring a number of penalties and spectacular free-kicks. He soon held cult hero status at The Valley.

His good form continued in 2012/13 in the Championship, when he was on target 11 times as the Addicks finished ninth.

The 2013/14 campaign opened for the Addicks at AFC Bournemouth and Kermorgant scored in a 1-2 defeat. His next strike came in the fourth match at home to his old club Leicester City, where his goal clinched the Addicks' first League win (2-1). His penalty in the next fixture at Watford secured a 1-1 draw.

As the Addicks struggled for form, the second win did not arrive until October, Kermorgant missed a number of games through injury and was often restricted to cameo appearances from the bench.

Come December and he was back on form, scoring at Bolton Wanderers in a 1-1 draw and then on Boxing Day against Brighton & Hove Albion where he netted the third goal in the 3-2 victory.

In January he turned his attention to the FA Cup when Oxford United visited

SE7 for a third round tie. The visitors were two up by half-time but a second-half comeback culminated in the Frenchman hitting an equaliser in a -2 draw. The replay at Oxford was more straight-forward as the Addicks cruised to a 3-0 victory with Kermorgant netting a brace.

Those goals were to be the last he scored for the Club as he was controversially sold to AFC Bournemouth for an undisclosed fee at the end of the January transfer window. It was a body blow to the Addicks as the Frenchman had become the heartbeat of the side, along with the likes of Johnnie Jackson. Talented midfielder Dale Stephens was also sold (to Brighton) so the squad was severely weakened and the Club would not recover from these actions for a number of seasons.

Despite Kermorgant's premature departure, he still finished as joint top scorer with eight goals. It would have been significantly more had he been allowed to stay in SE7.

He did well at AFC Bournemouth and helped them to win the Championship title in 2015 and promotion to the Premier League. However, he was used only as a substitute by the Cherries in the Premier League and in January 2016 he moved back to the Championship with Reading.

He was a success with the Royals too, and was part of the team that reached the Championship Play-off Final in 2017, where they cruelly lost on penalties to Huddersfield Town at Wembley. He spent one more season with the Berkshire club before returning to France in 2018 where he rejoined his first club, Vannes, where he wound down his career, retiring in April 2020 at the age of 38.

On his retirement the tributes to him from fans at Charlton, AFC Bournemouth and Reading bore testament to the excellent service he provided to those clubs.

Yann was a popular figure at The Valley and it was a privilege to see him wearing the red shirt for those two and half seasons.

Charlton Career:

Seasons: 2011/12 – 2013/14

Football League: 78+11A 28G

FA Cup: 4+1A 3G

League Cup: 0+1A 0G

Football League Trophy: 0+1A 0G

Total: 82+14A 31G

Marvin Sordell

Football League:	20+11A	7G
FA Cup:	1+1A	0G
League Cup:	1+1A	1G
Total	22+13A	8G

Marvin Sordell
CHARLTON ATHLETIC FC

Marvin Anthony Sordell

Born: Pinner, London, 17.2.1991

Career:
Fulham
Watford (FL 51+24A 21G)
Wealdstone (loan)
Tranmere Rovers (loan) (FL 6+2A 1G)
Bolton Wanderers (PL/FL 13+12A 4G)
Charlton Athletic (loan) (FL 20+11A 7G)
Burnley (PL/FL 2+15A 0G)
Colchester United (FL 19+2A 4G)
Coventry City (FL 18+2A 4G)
Burton Albion (FL 58+14A 9G)
Northampton Town (loan) (FL 5+3A 0G)

Honours:
England U20 – 1 cap - 1 goal (with Watford)
England U21 – 14 caps – 3 goals (with Watford & Bolton)
Great Britain – 3 caps in 2012 Olympics (with Bolton)

Marvin Sordell's career began in Fulham's academy before he moved to Watford's academy, where he was signed as a professional in July 2009.

The pacy striker had loan spells at Wealdstone and Tranmere Rovers while with the Hornets, and eventually established himself in their First Team. He was capped by England at U20 and U21 levels while at Vicarage Road and in January 2012 he moved to Premier League Bolton Wanderers in a £3m (=£3.5m) deal.

He struggled for consistent form with the Trotters and joined Charlton on loan for the 2013/14 season. His first goal for the Addicks came in the League Cup second round in August 2013 at Huddersfield Town, but his strike could not prevent a 2-3 defeat.

His first League goal came in October when he struck the equaliser in a 1-1 home draw with Nottingham Forest. He found himself on the bench for much of the campaign and he made 13 appearances from there over the course of the season.

He did not get on the scoresheet again until February when he found the net after only three minutes in the 1-2 reverse at Wigan Athletic, a match which the Addicks were winning up to the 88th minute.

By April, Charlton were desperate for points to avoid relegation and Sordell was on target in a much need 3-2 home victory over Yeovil Town.

Then came his finest hour at Sheffield Wednesday on Easter Monday. After only ten minutes the Addicks were 0-2 down when Sordell turned the game, scoring twice before the interval to level things at 2-2. He then completed his hat-trick in the second-half to secure a priceless 3-2 victory.

He scored in the next match too, at home to Blackburn Rovers, but that ended in a dismal 1-3 defeat.

Charlton had two matches left to save their skins and thankfully they won both, against Watford (3-1) and at Blackpool (3-0) to preserve their Championship status.

Sordell finished as joint top scorer with eight goals along with the now departed Yann Kermorgant, as the Addicks finished in 18th position.

In June 2014 he joined Premier League Burnley where he was mainly used as substitute, and in September 2015 he signed for Colchester United where he spent one season before joining Coventry City in July 2016.

In January 2017 he was on the move again, to Burton Albion, who were then in the Championship. January 2019 saw him join his last League club,

Northampton Town, on loan, and he finally retired from the game in July 2019 aged only 28, citing mental health issues as the main reason for his decision.

Marvin was undoubtedly an unfulfilled talent and failed to realise the potential he showed in his early career.

However, at Charlton he will be remembered for his Easter Monday 2014 hat-trick which was instrumental in saving the Club from relegation.

Charlton Career:

Season: 2013/14

Football League: 20+11A 7G

FA Cup: 1+1A 0G

League Cup: 1+1A 1G

Total: 22+13A 8G

2014/15   Igor Vetokele & Johann Berg Gudmundsson

Football League – Championship

Leading Scorers: Igor Vetokele & Johann Berg Gudmundsson

Igor Vetokele

Football League:	37+4A	11G
FA Cup:	0A	0G
League Cup:	0+2A	0G
Total	37+6A	11G

Igor Mavuba Vetokele

Born: Ostend, Belgium, 23.3.1992

Career:
KV Oostende
Gent
Cercle Brugge* (34+4A 9G)
FC Copenhagen* (31+13A 16G)
Charlton Athletic (FL 60+20A 16G)
Zulte Waregem (loan)* (5+9A 0G)
Sint-Truiden (loan)* (31+12A 11G)
KVC Westerlo* (16+2A 4G) - Up to and including 2019/20
* Domestic league record

Honours: - Up to and including 2019/20
Belgium U17 – 8 caps – 3 goals
Belgium U18 – 9 caps – 3 goals
Belgium U19 –17 caps – 2 goals
Belgium U21 – 14 caps – 4 goals
Angola Full International – 6 caps (4 caps with Charlton)
Danish Superliga champions medal 2012/13 (with FC Copenhagen)
Danish Superliga runners-up 2013/14 (with FC Copenhagen)
Danish Cup runners-up medal 2013/14 (with FC Copenhagen)

Belgian born striker Igor Vetokele started his career in the youth academies at KV Oostende and Gent. In 2011 he joined Cercle Brugge, who were managed by future Charlton boss Bob Peeters, and it was there that he made the breakthrough to first team football.

His impressive form caught the attention of Danish club FC Copenhagen who paid a fee of around £900,000 (=£1.07m) for his services in September 2012. Vetokele enjoyed a successful time in Denmark, helping his new club to win the Danish League in his first season, 2012/13, and finish as runners-up the following year. He also experienced European football, playing in both the Europa League and the Champions League.

Having been capped by Belgian at U17 through to U21 level, he opted to play for Angola in 2014 and won two full caps that year.

In June 2014 Vetokele was reunited with Bob Peeters who had been recently been appointed manager of Charlton. The Addicks paid an undisclosed fee, thought to be in the region of £2.4m (=£2.7m), and he was signed on a five year contract.

He made a blistering start to his career at The Valley in 2014/15, scoring five times in the opening five matches.

The opening match was at Brentford and Vetokele gave the Addicks the lead but a late goal from the Bees meant they had to settle for a 1-1 draw. The next match was won without the Belgian scoring but he was on target in the third match as the Addicks eased past Derby County 3-2 at The Valley. He then netted a 93rd minute equaliser at Huddersfield Town to secure a 1-1 draw and rounded off August with a brace at Brighton & Hove Albion which finished 2-2.

Charlton made a good start to the campaign and were undefeated in the opening 11 matches. Vetokele scored his sixth of the season in that 11th match, a 1-1 home draw with Birmingham City in October.

November saw him add two more to his total as he hit the equaliser at home to Sheffield Wednesday (1-1) and scored the winner at Reading (1-0).

Following that there was a dismal run if eight games without a win, a sequence of results which led to Bob Peeters being sacked in January. Guy Luzon was appointed manager soon afterwards but the winless run stretched to 13 before he managed to turn things around in February.

Vetokele's next strike was at home to Norwich City where the Addicks succumbed 2-3 in the last match of the winless sequence. He was then on target in two emphatic 3-0 victories against Brentford in SE7 and at Wigan Athletic, thus scoring in three consecutive matches.

That brought his total to 11 goals. He was unable to add to that in the remaining matches but still finished as joint top scorer with Johann Gudmundsson as the Addicks finished in 12th position in the Championship table.

After such an impressive first season, great things were expected of Vetokele in 2015/16. However, injuries limited him to only 11 starts in a dismal campaign for him and the Addicks which ended in relegation to League One.

In July 2016 he returned to Belgium on loan to Zulte Waregem before switching to Sint Truiden in January 2017, also on loan, where he stayed until the summer of 2018.

He then returned to Charlton to play under Lee Bowyer and was part of the squad which won promotion back to the Championship, via the play-offs, in 2018/19, scoring four times in his 12 League starts.

He was released by Charlton at the end of the season and returned to Belgium where he signed for KVC Westerlo for the 2019/20 campaign.

Igor became an almost instant fans favourite at The Valley due to his prolific start to the 2014/15 season. It is a shame that injuries then restricted his appearances and the Club's relegation saw him depart on loan for two seasons. At least he was able to return to play his part in restoring the Club back to the Championship in 2019.

Charlton Career:

Seasons: 2014/15 – 2015/16, 2018/19

Football League: 60+20A   16G

FA Cup: 0+1A   0G

League Cup: 0+3A   1G

Football League Trophy: 2A 1G

Total: 62+24A   18G

Johann Berg Gudmundsson

Football League:	38+3A	10G
FA Cup:	1A	1G
League Cup:	0+<u>2A</u>	<u>0G</u>
Total	39+5A	11G

Johann Berg Gudmundsson
CHARLTON ATHLETIC FC

Johann Berg Gudmundsson

Born: Reykjavik, Iceland, 27.10.1990

Career:
Breidablik (Iceland)
Chelsea
Fulham
Breidablik (Iceland)
AZ Alkmaar (Holland)* (68+51A 9G)
Charlton Athletic (FL 77+4A 16G)
Burnley (PL 67+29A 7G) - Up to and including 2019/20
* Domestic league record

Honours: - Up to and including 2019/20
Iceland U19 – 2 caps – 1 goal
Iceland U21 – 14 caps – 6 goals
Iceland Full International – 75 caps – 7 goals (20 caps with Charlton)
KNVB Cup winners' medal 2012/13 (with AZ Alkmaar)

Icelandic winger, Johann Berg Gudmundsson, developed in the youth academy of Breidablik in Iceland and also had spells in England with Fulham and Chelsea while studying in London.

He returned to Iceland and began his senior career with Breidablik in 2008 before being signed by Dutch club AZ Alkmaar in January 2009. He enjoyed a successful five years there which included winning the Dutch Cup with a victory over PSV Eindhoven in 2013. He played in the Europa League and also became an established Full international with Iceland.

In July 2014 he signed for Charlton, after his contract had expired at AZ Alkmaar, and was deployed on the wing where he used his deadly left foot to good effect. He was a dead-ball expert and went on to score with some spectacular free-kicks and long range strikes.

His first goal for the Addicks in 2014/15 came at Rotherham United in September in a 1-1 draw and he then scored a brace at Leeds United in another match which finished all-square (2-2).

His best strike came on Boxing Day at home to Cardiff City where his late long-range equaliser salvaged a point in a 1-1 draw. It was later voted Charlton's Goal of the Season.

In January he found the target in the FA Cup third round tie at home to Blackburn Rovers, where his equaliser proved not to be enough as the Addicks were eliminated 1-2.

A goal at Middlesbrough in February brought his total to six but it was only a consolation in a 1-3 defeat. He then opened the scoring at The Valley as Brentford were dispatched 3-0 and he did the same a few weeks later as Huddersfield Town were also defeated 3-0 in SE7.

In March, another 3-0 victory was chalked up at Blackpool with the Icelander netting his ninth of the campaign, and in April he was on target in successive games as he scored equalisers at home to Fulham (1-1) and at Sheffield Wednesday (1-1).

That brought his total to 11 goals and he finished an impressive first season in SE7 as joint top scorer with Igor Vetokele and was runner-up in the Player of the Year poll.

The Addicks finished mid-table in 12th position.

Charlton Career:

See Season 2015/16

2015/16   Johann Berg Gudmundsson

Football League – Championship

Leading Scorer: Johann Berg Gudmundsson

Football League:	39+1A	6G
FA Cup:	0A	0G
League Cup:	0+2A	0G
Total	39+3A	6G

Johann Berg Gudmundsson
CHARLTON ATHLETIC FC

Charlton made a promising start to the 2015/16 campaign and were undefeated in the opening four matches. The fourth game was a 2-1 home win over Hull City and it was Gudmundsson who clinched the points with a dramatic 98th minute winner.

The next match was at Wolverhampton Wanderers and the Icelander was on target again, putting the Addicks ahead in the second-half only for the hosts to score twice and inflict a 1-2 defeat.

That loss sparked a depressing 11 game winless run which culminated in Guy Luzon being sacked in October to be replaced by Karel Fraeye.

There was a brief respite in November with two consecutive victories but that proved to be a false dawn as another winless 11 game run followed. Fraeye was dismissed in January and Jose Riga became the third manager of the season to attempt to steer the Addicks to safety.

By the end of January, Charlton had only recorded five League wins and February was no better with only one point taken from five matches. Gudmundsson did score in one of those games, hitting the equaliser at Preston North End, before the Addicks predictably imploded to lose 1-2.

March saw an upturn in form as the Addicks won three of the next six matches and only lost once. Gudmundsson was on target in one of those victories when he netted the equaliser at home to Birmingham City which set up a 2-1 win.

However following that, the last six matches yielded only one victory, a run which finally condemned them to relegation. The Icelander was still producing his best in a struggling side and managed two more strikes before the season mercifully ended. He was on target in the 1-3 home defeat to Brighton & Hove Albion and also in the last victory of the season at Leeds United (2-1).

Charlton finished in 22nd position and were relegated to League One after four seasons in the Championship. The fact that Gudmundsson finished top scorer with a modest six goals highlighted the Addicks' lack of firepower as only 40 League goals were scored in total.

Gudmundsson's quality still shone through and it was no surprise when he left The Valley during the close season. Burnley had won the Championship title and it was they who signed him, for an undisclosed fee, in July 2016 as they returned to the Premier League.

Johann has gone on to establish himself as a valuable member of Burnley's Premier League squad and has also continued his international career with Iceland, playing in the finals of Euro 2016 and the FIFA World Cup 2018.

Charlton Career:

Seasons: 2014/15 – 2015/16

Football League: 77+4A   16G

FA Cup: 1A   1G

League Cup: 0+4A   0G

Total: 78+8A   17G

2016/17 Ricky Holmes

Football League – League One

Leading Scorer: Ricky Holmes

Football League: 31+4A 13G

FA Cup: 1A 0G

League Cup: 1A 0G

Football League Trophy: 1A 0G

Total 34+4A 13G

Ricky Lee Holmes

Born: Rochford, Essex, 19.6.1987

Career:
Southend United
Chelmsford City
Barnet (FL 72+19A 15G)
Portsmouth (FL 40+13A 2G)
Northampton Town (loan) (FL 4A 1G)
Northampton Town (FL 37+8A 13G)
Charlton Athletic (FL 53+5A 19G)
Sheffield United (FL 1+4A 0G)
Oxford United (loan) (FL 13+3A 3G)
Gillingham (loan) (FL 0A 0G)

Honours:
Isthmian League Premier Division champions medal 2007/08
(with Chelmsford City)
England C (Semi-pro) – 1 cap (with Chelmsford City)
FL League Two (Tier 4) Champions medal 2015/16
(with Northampton Town)

Ricky Holmes was born in Essex and started his career in Southend United's youth academy in 2002 before joining Chelmsford City's academy in 2004. It was at Chelmsford that he made his breakthrough to the first team in 2005 and he enjoyed a successful five years there, winning promotion to the Conference South in 2008, being voted their Player of the Year, winning an England 'C' cap and netting 67 goals for the Clarets.

He was on the radar of a number of Football League clubs and was eventually signed by League Two Barnet in June 2010. After three seasons he moved to Portsmouth, also in League Two, where he again won the Player of the Year award in 2014.

In January 2015, He joined Northampton Town on loan and impressed enough to be offered a permanent deal. He starred for the Cobblers as they won the League Two Championship in 2015/16, netting 11 goals (9 in the League) and was named in the League Two Team of the Year.

In June 2016, new Charlton manager, Russell Slade, signed Holmes for the Addicks for an undisclosed fee, thought to be in the region of £125,000 (=£137,000). He was Slade's first signing as he looked to assemble a squad capable of taking the Club back to the Championship at the first attempt.

Holmes was equally at home on the left-wing or playing behind the strikers in a "number 10 role" and had a penchant for scoring spectacular goals.

The Addicks made a slow start to the 2016/17 campaign and did not register their first win until the third match when two trademark strikes from Holmes secured a 3-0 victory over Shrewsbury Town in SE7.

The team struggled for consistency in the early months of the season with too many games being drawn, but one convincing win came in October when Coventry City were defeated 3-0 at The Valley with Holmes netting his third of the season.

By November there was still no sign of the team mounting a promotion challenge and Russell Slade was dismissed following another poor performance in a 0-3 defeat at Swindon Town.

Karl Robinson was appointed in his place but by this time Holmes was sidelined with a back injury, a condition that plagued him throughout his career.

He missed ten matches and did not make another start until February at home to Fleetwood Town where he duly scored in the 1-1 draw. He was on target in the next match too as the Addicks drew yet again (1-1) at AFC

Wimbledon who equalised in the 92nd minute.

That month saw not a single win in the seven matches played. That trend seemed to be changing at Shrewsbury Town in the last match in February as Holmes netted a hat-trick. The Addicks somehow still contrived to lose 3-4.

In March he gave the Addicks an early lead at Sheffield United only for them to slump to another defeat (1-2). Only one win was registered in 14 matches between the start of February and early April as the Addicks found themselves consigned to mid-table.

However, the last five matches in April saw the Addicks finally hit form, winning four and drawing one. Holmes was on target in those four victories, at home to Southend United (2-1) and Gillingham (3-0), at Chesterfield (2-1) and in the final game at home to Swindon Town (3-0).

That brought his total to 13 goals, all in the League. Had he not missed such a large part of the season through injury it would have been many more. Charlton would have prospered too instead of finishing in a disappointing 13th position.

Holmes was, not surprisingly, voted Player of the Year.

He continued with the Addicks for the 2017/18 season and had scored another six goals by the time Sheffield United came calling in the January transfer window. The Blades were managed by Chris Wilder, who was manager of Northampton Town when they won the League Two title, with Holmes playing a starring role.

Wilder signed him for an undisclosed fee, thought to be around £400,000, and Holmes had the opportunity to continue his career in the Championship. However, his back injury prevented him from making an impact at Bramall Lane and he only managed to play a handful of games.

In August 2018 he had a loan spell at Oxford United, under former Addicks boss Karl Robinson, and in January 2019 he had another loan spell at

Gillingham but his injury prevented him from making any appearances for them.

In May 2020, Holmes finally called time on his career and announced his retirement.

Ricky Holmes was only at The Valley for one and half seasons but he was immensely popular during that time, scoring some spectacular goals and he certainly provided value for money.

Charlton Career:

Seasons: 2016/17 – 2017/18

Football League: 53+5A 19G

FA Cup: 3A 0G

League Cup: 1A 0G

Football League Trophy: 1+1A 0G

Total: 58+6A 19G

2017/18   Josh Magennis

Football League – League One

Leading Scorer: Josh Magennis

Football League:	37+5A	10G
FA Cup:	1A	0G
League Cup:	0+1A	0G
Football League Trophy:	1A	0G
Play-Offs:	2A	0G
Total	41+6A	10G

Joshua Brendan David Magennis

Born: Bangor, Northern Ireland, 15.8.1990

Career:
Bryansburn Rangers
Lisburn Distillery
Glentoran
Cardiff City (FL 1+8A 0G)
Grimsby Town (loan) (FL 1+1A 0G)
Aberdeen (SL 42+63A 10G)
St Mirren (loan) (SL 7+6A 0G)
Kilmarnock (SL 70+2A 18G)
Charlton Athletic (FL 73+8A 20G)
Bolton Wanderers (FL 29+13A 4G)
Hull City (FL 20+9A 4G) - Up to and including 2019/20

Honours: - Up to and including 2019/20
Northern Ireland U17 – 2 caps – 0G
Northern Ireland U19 – 6 caps – 1G
Northern Ireland U21 – 17 caps – 4G
Northern Ireland Full International – 50 caps – 7G
(15 caps – 3G with Charlton)

Josh Magennis began his career as a goalkeeper in his native Northern Ireland and it was in this capacity that he joined Cardiff City from Glentoran in 2007. It was while at Cardiff that he made the switch to striker and was signed as a professional in April 2009.

In October 2009 he had a loan spell at Grimsby Town before making a permanent move to Aberdeen in July 2010 in order to get regular first team football. During his time at Pittodrie, he also had a spell playing at right-back, to further endorse his versatility, but it was as a striker that he was mainly deployed and he began to establish himself as a Full international with Northern Ireland.

A loan move to St Mirren in January 2014 preceded a permanent deal with Kilmarnock in July 2014. He spent two seasons at Rugby Park before joining Charlton for an undisclosed fee, thought to be in the region of £270,000, in August 2016.

In his first season at The Valley, 2016/17, the powerful striker scored 10 goals and was the Club's second highest scorer behind Ricky Holmes with 13.

The 2017/18 campaign saw the Addicks make a promising start, winning five of their opening six matches. Magennis was on target in three of those victories, scoring his first goal of the season in the 4-1 demolition of Northampton Town at The Valley, at Rotherham United in a 2-0 triumph, and in the 2-1 win over Southend United back in SE7.

His next strike was an equaliser in the 1-1 home draw with Bury in late September but he had to wait until November for his next goal which came at The Valley in another draw, 2-2 with MK Dons.

The Addicks' good early season form seemed to evaporate in mid-November and they went eight League matches without a win before tasting victory again in early January when they won three in a row.

February saw the Irishman add three more to his total when he netted at home to Oxford United (2-3) and Bradford City (1-1) and at MK Dons in a

2-1 victory. That was the only win in a run of eight games and the Addicks started to slide into mid-table.

Manager Karl Robinson left the Club by mutual consent in March to join Oxford United, leaving his assistant, Lee Bowyer, in temporary charge.

There was an immediate reaction and Bowyer rekindled the Club's play-off aspirations with three straight wins. The most eye-catching was the 4-0 thrashing handed out to Northampton Town at Sixfields where Magennis hit his ninth goal to the campaign.

Bowyer oversaw the last ten matches of the season, six of which were won, with Magennis again on target at Shrewsbury Town in a 2-0 victory, a result which helped to propel the Addicks to 6th position and a place in the Play-offs.

Shrewsbury were again the opponents in the Play-off semi-final but the Addicks came up short, losing both legs 0-1, and it was the Shrews that advanced to the final.

Magennis finished as top scorer with ten goals, replicating his total of the previous season.

Although he hadn't managed to get the Addicks promoted to the Championship, he did find himself playing in that division the following season. Bolton Wanderers signed him in July 2018 for an undisclosed fee, thought to be around £200,000.

He spent one season with the Trotters but following their relegation and fall into administration, he signed for Hull City in August 2019 to continue his career in the Championship. That only lasted one season as the Tigers were also relegated to League One at the end of 2019/20.

Josh Magennis is still with Hull and they will be looking to him to score the goals to take them back to the Championship.

He did well in his two seasons at The Valley, hitting double figures in both campaigns and has now racked up 50 international appearances for Northern Ireland.

Charlton Career:

Seasons: 2016/17 – 2017/18

Football League: 73+8A 20G

FA Cup: 3A 0G

League Cup: 0+1A 0G

Football League Trophy: 1A 0G

Play-Offs: 2A 0G

Total: 79+9A 20G

2018/19 Lyle Taylor

Football League – League One

Leading Scorer: Lyle Taylor

Football League:	41A	21G
FA Cup:	1A	3G
League Cup:	0A	0G
Football League Trophy:	0A	0G
Play-offs:	<u>3A</u>	<u>1G</u>
Total	45A	25G

Lyle Taylor
CHARLTON ATHLETIC FC

Lyle James Alfred Taylor

Born: Greenwich, London, 29.3.1990

Career:
Glebe
Staines Town
Millwall (FL 0A 0G)
Eastbourne Borough (loan)
Concord Rangers
AFC Bournemouth (FL 9+20A 0G)
Lewes (loan)
Hereford United (loan) (FL 6+2A 2G)
Woking (loan)
Falkirk (SL 34A 24G)
Sheffield United (FL 9+11A 2G)
Partick Thistle (loan) (SL 17+3A 7G)
Scunthorpe United (FL 11+7A 3G)
Partick Thistle (loan) (SL 10+5A 3G)
AFC Wimbledon (FL 116+15A 44G)
Charlton Athletic (FL 58+5A 32G) - Up to and including 2019/20
Nottingham Forest (signed 15/8/2020)

Honours: - Up to and including 2019/20
Montserrat Full International – 6 caps – 1 goal (3 caps with Charlton)
FL League Two (Tier 4) play-off winners' medal 2016
(with AFC Wimbledon)
FL League One (Tier 3) play-off winners' medal 2019 (with Charlton)

Lyle Taylor was born in Greenwich and started his professional with Millwall in 2007. He had a loan spell at Eastbourne Borough but was unable to break into the Lions' first team and was released in May 2009. He then signed for Essex club, Concord Rangers, in July 2009 and in his first season in the Isthmian League he hit 34 goals in 42 matches.

That attracted the attention of Football League clubs and AFC Bournemouth signed him in August 2010 to bring him back into the full-time game. He had loan spells at Lewes, Hereford United and Woking but ultimately was unable to get regular game time with the Cherries and he was released in May 2012.

His next move was to Scotland where he joined Falkirk in July 2012. In his first season with the Bairns he hit 24 goals in the Scottish First Division (tier 2) and once again English clubs were alerted to his talent.

In the 2013 close season, Sheffield United signed him for an undisclosed fee, thought to be around £225,000, to bring him back to the Football League. However, that move did not work out and again he was unable to command a regular starting place with the Blades in League One, not helped by a managerial change during the season. He then found himself out on loan again, back in Scotland, with Partick Thistle for the remainder of the 2013/14 campaign.

Despite being quite successful with the Jags in the Scottish Premiership, when he returned to Bramall Lane in the summer he found himself surplus to requirements. He therefore moved to Scunthorpe United in League Two for an undisclosed fee in June 2014 but in February 2015 he returned to Partick Thistle on loan for the remainder of the season. He also won the first of his Full international caps for Montserrat in March 2015.

In July 2015, Taylor made what turned out to be the most significant move of his nomadic career, joining AFC Wimbledon for an undisclosed fee. In his first season with them in League Two he scored 23 goals as they won promotion via the Play-offs. His tally included one in the Wembley Play-off Final against Plymouth Argyle which was won 2-0.

He continued to score in League One, hitting 10 in 2016/17 and 14 in 2017/18 to bring his total to 44 League goals, setting a new club record.

He allowed his contract to run down and became a free agent in the summer of 2018. That was when Charlton stepped in to sign him in June 2018 as a replacement for the departed Josh Magennis. Lee Bowyer was keen to aquire Taylor as he had scored three times against the Addicks the previous season.

It was hoped that Taylor would provide the goals that had been lacking in the Addicks' previous attempts to escape from League One.

He got off to a promising start in the 2018/19 campaign, scoring a penalty at Sunderland on the opening day to give the Addicks the lead, but they ultimately lost 1-2 to a sickening 96th minute winner from the hosts.

Shrewsbury Town were then defeated 2-1 at The Valley with Taylor on target again. The winning goal came from Karlan Grant who was to form a formidable partnership with Taylor.

The extrovert Taylor soon became a fans favourite with his goals and dyed blonde hair (or pink when he was raising awareness for Cancer Research). In September he scored in three successive victories, at Southend United (2-1), home to Wycombe Wanderers (3-2) and at Bradford City (2-0).

In October, the Addicks' form dipped but Taylor kept on scoring. He was on target at Scunthorpe United (3-5) and at home to Coventry City (1-2) and Oxford United (1-1), the latter two strikes coming from the penalty spot.

The results improved again in November and he scored from the spot again at Walsall to set up a 2-0 win. This was quickly followed by a hat-trick in an FA Cup first round replay in SE7 when Mansfield Town were dismantled 5-0.

His 13th goal came in December against his former club, AFC Wimbledon, in a 2-0 Valley victory. On New Year's Day he and Grant both scored in the opening eight minutes at home to Walsall, Taylor converting another penalty in the 2-1 triumph.

That win triggered an incredible run which saw the Addicks lose only twice in the remaining 20 matches.

A resounding 3-0 victory at Shrewsbury Town saw Taylor net goal 15 but in the next match, at home to Accrington Stanley, he was sent off as the Addicks just edged home 1-0 with a last minute Grant penalty.

Taylor was therefore suspended for the next three matches and, by the time he returned, his strike partner Grant had been sold to Premier League Huddersfield Town.

In March, Taylor netted another three goals. The first came in a vital 2-1 home win over promotion rivals Portsmouth and a few days later he scored a penalty as Burton Albion were beaten by the same score in SE7. He then netted the only goal of the game as the Addicks edged past Bradford City 1-0 at The Valley.

A week later he opened the scoring at Plymouth Argyle as the Addicks romped to another win (2-0). The next visitors to SE7 were league leaders Luton Town who were on a long unbeaten run. It was the Hatters who led at the break but Taylor turned the game in the second half, scoring twice, once from the penalty spot, as the Addicks triumphed 3-1.

His goal tally now stood at 21 but there was more to come. Next up was a visit to Oxford United which saw Taylor net another penalty to give the visitors the lead in a rare defeat (1-2).

However, the Addicks signed off with three successive victories and Taylor was on target in two of them, both at The Valley. Scunthorpe United were thrashed 4-0 with Taylor netting the fourth, and in the final League match Rochdale were beaten by the same score with Taylor hitting the third goal.

That result clinched third position and a place in the Play-offs.

Charlton had to play sixth placed Doncaster Rovers in the semi-final. The first leg was at Doncaster and Taylor, who had already scored 24 goals, made it 25 after 32 minutes as the Addicks won 2-1. The second leg at The Valley was a dramatic night as despite the hosts extending their aggregate lead to 3-1, Doncaster hit back to win 3-2 on the night, after extra time, to square the tie at 4-4. It therefore went to penalties and the Addicks held their nerve to win the shoot-out 4-3, with Taylor netting his spot kick in the process.

The Play-off Final at Wembley against Sunderland was another tight affair with a dramatic ending. Patrick Bauer's last minute goal for the Addicks clinched a 2-1 win and promotion back to the Championship.

Lyle Taylor's 25 goal haul was the biggest by a Charlton player for 19 years, equaling Andy Hunt's total in 1999/2000 when the Addicks won promotion to the Premier League as First Division Champions.

Taylor had become the team's talisman and, not surprisingly, was voted Player of the Year.

Charlton Career:

See Season 2019/20

2019/20 Lyle Taylor & Macauley Bonne

Football League – Championship

Leading Scorers: Lyle Taylor & Macauley Bonne

Lyle Taylor

Football League:	17+5A	11G
FA Cup:	0A	0G
League Cup:	0A	0G
Total	17+5A	11G

Lyle Taylor
CHARLTON ATHLETIC FC

Having enjoyed such a stellar season and winning promotion, the question was could Lyle Taylor replicate his strike rate at the higher level in what was to be his first ever season in the Championship ?

That question was answered emphatically in the first six matches in which the Addicks were undefeated and Taylor netted five goals.

The first match was at Blackburn Rovers and Taylor scored the second goal to seal a 2-1 victory. Charlton then eased past Stoke City 3-1 at The Valley with Taylor opening the scoring before a visit to Barnsley where he dispatched a penalty in a 2-2 draw. It was then four goals in four matches as he was on target back in SE7 against Nottingham Forest in a 1-1 draw. His fifth goal came at Reading where he converted another penalty in a 2-0 win.

Five goals in six games was a great start for Taylor and the future looked bright both for him and for Charlton. Then disaster struck. While away on international duty with Monserrat in September, he suffered a knee injury which sidelined him for over three months, causing him to miss 15 League matches, basically a third of the season.

Without Taylor's goals and with a growing injury list going into autumn and winter, the Addicks struggled and slipped down the Championship table. A win against Derby County (3-0) in mid-October was the only victory recorded for two months, the next one not arriving until Boxing Day.

Taylor did return to action in late December and scored in the 2-2 draw at Queens Park Rangers and he also netted a penalty when coming off the bench at Derby County in a 1-2 defeat.

By February, he was starting games on a regular basis again and provided vital goals in three crucial victories in what was by now a relegation battle. Fellow strugglers Barnsley were beaten 2-1 at The Valley with Taylor hitting the first goal. He then netted the only goal at Nottingham Forest in a 1-0 win and then scored a brace, one a penalty, in a vital 3-1 home victory over fellow strugglers Luton Town.

However, the next three matches were lost, with the Addicks failing to score in any of them and they slipped into the bottom three. If that wasn't bad enough, the growing coronavirus pandemic brought life, and football, to a shuddering halt. No matches were played from early March until the resumption on 20th June, but even then all matches were played behind closed doors with fans excluded on safety grounds.

As the Addicks returned to training in preparation for their remaining nine League matches, came the news that they would have to do it all without Lyle Taylor. He elected not to play because he didn't want to risk injury and jeopardise a big money move at the end of the campaign. His contract was due to expire at the end of June but he even declined to play in the three fixtures up to that point.

Charlton were looking to get themselves out of the relegation zone in the remaining games and without their main source of goals (Taylor had scored 11 times in only 17 starts) it began to look a forlorn hope, and so it proved.

Taylor did get his move, joining Championship club Nottingham Forest in August 2020 on a free transfer. Relegation could not totally be blamed on him but his refusal to play was certainly a major factor. Up to that point his popularity at the Club knew no bounds and it was such a sad end to his two years at The Valley. It was certainly not the best way to leave a club.

Charlton Career:

Seasons: 2018/19 – 2019/20

Football League: 58+5A 32G

FA Cup: 1A 3G

League Cup: 0A 0G

Play-Offs: 3A 1G

Total: 62+5A 36G

Macauley Bonne

Football League:	26+7A	11G
FA Cup:	0A	0G
League Cup:	<u>1A</u>	<u>0G</u>
Total	27+7A	11G

Macauley Bonne
CHARLTON ATHLETIC FC

Macauley Miles Bonne

Born: Ipswich, Suffolk, 26.10.1995

Career:
Ipswich Town
Norwich City
Colchester United (FL 19+56A 7G)
Lincoln City (loan) (NL 5+2A 1G)
Woking (loan) (NL 5+2A 0G)
Leyton Orient (NL 89+1A 45G)
Charlton Athletic (FL 26+7A 11G) - Up to and including 2019/20
Queens Park Rangers (signed 2/10/2020)

Honours: - Up to and including 2019/20
Zimbabwe U23 – 1 cap - 1G (with Colchester United)
Zimbabwe Full international – 2 caps (with Leyton Orient)
National League Champions medal 2018/19 (with Leyton Orient)
FA Trophy runners-up medal 2018/19 (with Leyton Orient)

Macauley Bonne started his career in the youth academy of his hometown club Ipswich Town before having spells in the academies at Norwich City and Colchester United. It was at Colchester that he made his breakthrough having been a prolific scorer for their youth teams. He made his Football League debut for them in October 2013, just before his 18th birthday.

He had loan spells in the National League with Lincoln City (September 2016) and Woking (January 2017) before signing for Leyton Orient for an undisclosed fee July 2017. He hit 22 goals in the National League for The O's in 2017/18 and 23 in 2018/19 as Orient finished as champions and returned to the Football League. They were also runners-up in the FA Trophy.

Charlton signed Bonne from Orient for a fee of £200,000 in June 2019. The idea was to develop him gradually but the injury situation at the Club resulted in him getting a lot more game time in the Championship than was planned.

He started the season on the bench and made a couple of appearances from there. The injury to Lyle Taylor in September opened up more opportunities for Bonne and he made his first League start against Leeds United at The Valley. He took his chance, scoring the only goal as the Addicks triumphed 1-0.

He became a fixture in the team for the next two months and in October he scored at Fulham (2-2), home to Derby County in an empathic 3-0 victory, at Bristol City in a 1-2 defeat, and at West Bromwich Albion which finished 2-2. He had now scored five times in his first six starts.

November was a dire month for the Addicks with only a single point being gained from the five matches. Bonne did manage a consolation goal in one of them, netting against Sheffield Wednesday in a 1-3 home defeat.

Taylor returned to fitness in December so it was hoped that the two would form an effective partnership.

On Boxing Day, Bonne was instrumental in ending an 11 match winless streak when he scored a brace as Bristol City were defeated 3-2 in SE7. But in January he succumbed to injury himself, missing seven matches and only returning to the team shortly before the season's shutdown due to the coronavirus pandemic.

By this time he had netted eight goals and with Taylor's decision not to play when the season resumed in June, Charlton's goal-scoring hopes were heaped onto Bonne's inexperienced shoulders.

In the event he did reasonably well, scoring three times in nine matches to equal Taylor's total of 11.

The Addicks commenced their mini nine game season with two wins and a draw to move out of the relegation places. But they lost the next three, despite Bonne giving them the lead at promotion hopefuls Brentford where the hosts hit back to inflict a 1-2 defeat.

The next two matches were drawn and Bonne scored in both of them, firstly at Birmingham City (1-1) and then at home to Wigan Athletic, where he scored in the last minute to secure a precious point in a 2-2 draw.

That result at least gave the Addicks some hope of avoiding the drop as they headed to Leeds United who had just been confirmed as champions. In the event it was not a happy evening but even after the 0-4 defeat they were still safe until Barnsley scored an unlikely winner at Brentford in added time to leave the Addicks in 22nd position, the last of the relegation places.

So after only one season in the Championship, the Club returned to League One. Macauley Bonne had done well however, making the transition from the National League to three levels higher and netting 11 goals.

He started the 2020/21 campaign at The Valley but his performances had not gone unnoticed and he moved to Queens Park Rangers in the extended transfer window, signing for them in October 2020 for an undisclosed fee, estimated at £2m.

Disappointing as it was to see another striker leave the Club, it was good business for Charlton and it gave Bonne the opportunity to continue his career in the Championship.

Charlton Career: Up to and including 2019/20

Season: 2019/20

Football League: 26+7A 11G

FA Cup: 0A 0G

League Cup: 1A 0G

Total: 27+7A 11G

About the Author

John Farrell was born in Petts Wood, Kent in December 1949.

He attended his first Charlton Athletic match at The Valley in August 1961 versus Stoke City. The match ended 2-2 and his life was never quite the same again.

He stuck loyally with Charlton, following them through thick and thin. It was of course mainly thin in the Sixties and Seventies but he eventually became a season-ticket holder in 1986 and he still holds one to this day.

He played football in the South London Alliance for 17 years while pursuing his career as a geophysicist in the oil exploration industry and studying for a degree with the Open University. Later he also worked for Philips Electronics.

Throughout that time, Charlton Athletic and The Valley were always a constant backdrop to his life.

He is now retired and lives by the sea at Selsey in West Sussex but he still manages to make it to The Valley for the majority of home games.

By the same author:

Valley Heroes – Part 1
Charlton Athletic's Leading Goalscorers
Seasons 1920/21 – 1968/69

Published on Amazon – November 2019

Bibliography

The following publications have been used as reference and to check and verify statistics:

The PFA Premier & Football League Players' Records 1946-2015 by Barry J. Hugman, G2 Entertainment 2015.

The Valiant 500 written & published by Colin Cameron 1991.

Home & Away with Charlton Athletic 1920-2004 by Colin Cameron, published by Colin Cameron & Rick Everitt 2003.

The Essential History of Charlton Athletic by Paul Clayton, Headline Book Publishing 2001.

A Record of Post-War Scottish League Players 1946/47-2009/10 (CD Rom) by John Litster, Scottish Football Historian Magazine 2011.

Charlton Athletic Football Club Official Handbooks

Printed in Poland
by Amazon Fulfillment
Poland Sp. z o.o., Wrocław